I love me,
I love me not...

A STUDY OF THE CHRISTIAN WOMAN'S SELF-ESTEEM

by
Rosemary Whittle McKnight

21ST CENTURY CHRISTIAN

2809 Granny White Pike
Nashville, Tennessee 37204

You are a wonderful,
worthy and loveable person.

Appreciate that about yourself.

No one has been,
or ever will be,
quite like you.

You are an individual,
an original,
and all those things that make you
uniquely you
are deserving of love
and praise.

—PETER A. WILLIAMS

acknowledgements

MY HEARTFELT THANKS & APPRECIATION GO TO:
Gary McKnight, my husband, for all his help and encouragement;

Mrs. Sue Mitchell, for typing the manuscript;

Mr. Tom Estes, for challenging me to write this book;

Ms. Karon Hightower, for editing my unskilled writing.

Lakewood Church of Christ Ladies' Bible Class, Montgomery, Alabama, for participating as a pilot class for this material;

The 210 women who participated in the self-esteem survey.

Scripture quotations are from the *New International Version* unless otherwise indicated.

a note to teachers

The members of your class will not improve their self-esteem by merely reading this book or hearing lectures on its contents. Their self-esteem will improve as they learn to encourage each other and meet one another's needs. I highly recommend that you use the activities listed at the end of each chapter. You may wish to develop other activities that meet the needs of your class. Encourage each member of the class to participate in discussions and activities. Every class member is important and can contribute something worthwhile.

Introduction

In 1980 I read Dr. James Dobson's book *What Wives Wish Their Husbands Knew About Women*. Dr. Dobson had conducted a survey to determine the sources of depression in women. The survey revealed that low self-esteem was the most troubling problem for women who completed the questionnaire. These women were saying they had feelings of inadequacy, lack of confidence, and worthlessness.

I was shocked when I read this. I thought, surely this can't be true among Christian women. If anyone has a reason to feel good about themselves, Christians certainly should.

I began listening more closely and watching my sisters in Christ, and I learned that, for many, low self-esteem is a problem. It often shows its effects in church work. Many women lack the confidence to be involved in personal evangelism or feel inadequate to teach a class. What a pity this is when God has given us every reason to be confident and feel worthy. I believe a good self-esteem does not begin with "self" at all, but it is based on God and what He has done for us.

The purpose of this book is to help Christian women develop a better self-esteem by examining things that destroy self-esteem, as well as things that build self-esteem. The contents are based on the results of a survey I conducted among 210 women who are members of the church of Christ. I am grateful to those who participated in this survey and also to those who have encouraged me to write this book.

I pray that as you read and discuss the chapters ahead, you will come to have a better self-esteem and, as a result, you will be a more confident servant for God.

table Of Contents

1

How Christian Women Feel About Themselves

Recently, a scene on *The Dukes Of Hazard* showed the deputy of Hazzard driving his patrol car and picking the petals off a daisy saying, "She loves me. She loves me not." He was trying to see how Daisy Duke felt about him. He was hoping to find the answer in a flower.

How others feel about us is important. It affects the way we feel about ourselves. How do you feel about yourself? "I love me. I love me not..." Do we need to go back to the daisy to find out?

The way we feel about ourselves is our self-esteem or self-concept. Jesus taught in Luke 10:27, "Thou shalt love thy neighbor *as thyself* (KJV)." Jesus knew that our love for others is an expression of how much we love ourselves. He was telling us we will have difficulty loving others if we don't have a proper respect and love for ourselves. How much do you love yourself?

I mentioned in the introduction that this book is a result of my reaction to Dr. James Dobson's book *What Wives Wish Their Husbands Knew About Women*. Dr. Dobson's survey of seventy-five women revealed the number-one source of depression in women is low self-esteem. That means many women are saying, "I love me not."

What Is Low Self-Esteem?

Low self-esteem, simply stated, is the inability to feel good about yourself. It is usually characterized by feelings of inadequacy, worthlessness, and a lack of self-confidence. Women with a low self-esteem may seem healthy, happy and content outwardly, but inwardly they feel a sense of personal inferiority and self-doubt. They have a hard time accepting compliments. They may accept unworthy labels for themselves such as "clumsy," "silly," "chubby," "dummy," etc.

Dr. Dobson describes women with a low self-esteem in the following way:

> It is sitting alone in a house during the quiet afternoon hours, wondering why you have no "real" friends. It is longing for someone to talk to, soul to soul, but knowing there is no such person worthy of your trust. It is the feeling that "they wouldn't like me if they knew the real me." It is becoming terrified when speaking to a group of your peers, and feeling like a fool when you get home. It is wondering why other people have so much more talent and ability than you do. It is feeling incredibly ugly and sexually unattractive. It is admitting that you have become a failure as a wife and mother. It is disliking everything about yourself and wishing, constantly wishing, you could be someone else. It is feeling unloved and unlovable and lonely and sad. It is lying in bed after the family is asleep, pondering the vast emptiness inside and longing for unconditional love. It is intense self-pity. It is reaching up in the darkness to remove a tear from the corner of your eye. It is depression!

Women with a low self-esteem often disguise their feelings by being very superficial. They have difficulty opening up to others and may come across as being very shy or quiet. Withdrawal and anger are two of the most familiar responses to inferior feelings. Neither are very healthy — physically or spiritually.

What Is High Self-Esteem?

High self-esteem is *not* a noisy conceit, a boastful spirit, or a self-righteous attitude as some may think. It is a quiet sense of self-respect and a feeling of self-worth. High self-esteem includes the ability to love yourself and to give and accept love from others. It is self-confidence in your abilities and talents, whatever they may be.

Women with a high self-esteem tend to have fewer illnesses. They are happier, more successful and make better decisions. Most even have a better family life than those with low self-esteem. Women with high self-esteem usually are more open and communicate well in a group. They are more likely to volunteer to do a job or to take a leadership role than women with low self-esteem. Women with high self-esteem show self-respect by taking care of themselves physically and mentally and by developing good spiritual and social attitudes. High self-esteem includes a feeling of security, significance and competence.

Why Study Self-Esteem?

Is our self-esteem important to God? I believe it is. When God made man, He made him in His image (Genesis 1:27). That made man special from the beginning. God has met our physical needs (Philippians 4:19). Even more importantly, God sacrificed His son Jesus and gave us the church and the Bible to meet our spiritual needs. He has given us as Christians every reason to feel good about ourselves because of His love for us. How do you think it makes God feel if He sees that after all He has done for us, we don't love or respect ourselves?

A study of self-esteem is important because self-esteem affects every area of our lives as Christians.

1. Our self-esteem affects our feelings toward ourselves. A woman with low self-esteem does not view herself as God does. Her self-pity focuses her attention on herself rather than others. She is too critical of herself and does not put her talents to use because she fears the criticism of others.

On the other hand, a Christian woman with high self-esteem draws her self-confidence from God (Philippians 4:13). She does not see herself as perfect or even great, but she knows she is special in God's eyes.

2. Our self-esteem affects our home. A woman with high self-esteem is better equipped to build the self-esteem of those in her family. Like the woman of Proverbs 31, she seeks to meet her family's needs and be a complement to her husband. She is hospitable and has confidence in her abilities as a housekeeper, wife, mother and friend. A woman with high self-esteem is more likely to view her home as a very special, God-given place and she desires to make it special for others.

3. Our self-esteem affects our relationship with the church. Almost any minister will tell you this is true. A woman with high self-esteem is more likely to become involved in various programs of her congregation and teach a Bible class. She recognizes what her talents are and seeks to use them for the Lord.

Women with low self-esteem are often very talented and creative, but they lack the confidence and initiative to put their talents to work. Like the man who hid his talent (Luke 19:11-27), they may not use their talents because they fear criticism or failure. Women with low self-esteem compare themselves with others and think, "Let her do it. She can do a better job than I can."

4. Our self-esteem affects our outreach to the lost. Women with a low self-esteem often feel like they could never teach the lost. They leave personal work up to the preachers and elders. They hold back from talking to their friends about their souls or inviting them to church because they fear rejection. Women with low self-esteem may stay away from religious discussions because they lack confidence in their ability to answer questions or defend their beliefs.

Women with high self-esteem, on the other hand, are more confident as soul winners. It is not necessarily because they care more about the lost. Their confidence is from God (II Corinthians 3:4-6). They recognize what God has done for them and are eager to share it with others.

We want to study self-esteem in this book because improving our self-esteem can improve our lives as Christians. We can become both more competent and more confident servants of God. That is our goal!

We do not want to improve our self-esteem merely to boost our egos. Hopefully, a better self-esteem will cause us to think less about our needs and desires and more about others. As our self-esteem improves we should be better equipped to serve God and to improve self-esteem in others.

How Do Christian Women Feel About Themselves?

We mentioned earlier that Dr. James Dobson's survey revealed the number one source of depression in women is low self-esteem. When I read that, I thought that this may be true among women in the world but surely not among Christian women. If anyone has a reason to have high self-esteem, it is the Christian woman!

The subject of the Christian woman's self-esteem stayed on my mind for two and a half years. I finally decided to find out for myself how Christian women felt about themselves. I was not out to disprove Dr. Dobson. I merely wanted to see if the Christian's self-esteem is different from women who are not Christians. I also wanted to see what Christian women considered to be self-esteem builders and destroyers in their lives.

Below is a copy of a questionniare that I developed. It was completed by women in churches of Christ and Christian colleges in seven states. They ranged in age from eighteen to eighty. Two hundred-ten women responded to the survey.

Look at the questionnaire and fill in your answers. (The term "self-concept" is used rather than "self-esteem." These terms are often used interchangeably.)

QUESTIONNAIRE

Please answer the following questions very honestly.

1. On a scale of 1 to 10 rate your own self-concept. (Circle one number.)

   VERY POOR   EXCELLENT
   1   2   3   4   5   6   7   8   9   10

2. Which of the following has had the geatest influence on helping you have a good self-concept: (Rate your top three answers.)

_____ good family background

_____ good relationship with God

_____ intelligence, competence, education

_____ appearance, beauty

_____ financial security

_____ acceptance and security

_____ present family situation

_____ praise and encouragement from others

_____ other (specify) _____

3. Which of the following has had the greatest influence on causing you to have a poor self-concept: (Rate your top three answers.)

_____ early family background

_____ poor relationship with God

_____ the world's values

_____ criticism, lack of encouragement

_____ present family situation

_____ guilt, anxiety, and fear

_____ rejection

_____ appearance

_____ other (specify) _____

4. What person or people have contributed the most to help you build a good self-concept: (Rate your top two answers.)

_____ parents   _____ non-Christian friends

_____ husband   _____ media (TV, magazines, etc.)

_____ children   _____ associates at work or school

_____ Christian friends   _____ other (specify) _____

5. What person or people have contributed the most to cause you to have a poor self-concept: (Rate your top two answers.)

_____ parents   _____ non-Christian friends

_____ husband   _____ media

_____ children   _____ associates at work or school

_____ Christian friends   _____ other (specify) _____

6. I engage in *personal* prayer and Bible study:
   ____ daily
   ____ several times a week
   ____ weekly
   ____ seldom
   ____ never

7. Your age in years: ☐ under 20 ☐ 20-40 ☐ 40-60 ☐ 60 +

8. ☐ single   ☐ married   ☐ widowed   ☐ divorced

9. Occupation_____

I compiled the results of the survey and drew some interesting conclusions. (The detailed results are listed in the Appendix at the conclusion of the book.) Here is how Christian women feel about themselves:

1. The majority of Christian women have a high self-esteem. Sixty percent of the women surveyed rated their self-concept as seven or above.

2. A good relationship with God has the most significant influence toward building a good self-concept. Early family background and praise and encouragement from others are also important self-esteem builders.

3. The influences that most often destroy the Christian woman's self-concept are guilt, anxiety, fear and criticism or lack of encouragement.

4. The people who contribute the most toward building a good self-concept are parents, Christian friends and husbands.

5. Non-Christian friends, the media, and our associates at work or school contribute the most to causing a poor self-concept.

6. Personal prayer and Bible study go hand-in-hand with the Christian woman's high self-concept. Ninety percent of those who rated their self-concept as eight or above engage in prayer and Bible study at least several times a week.

7. Age, marital status, or occupation (student, homemaker, or work outside the home) does not have a significant influence on the Christian woman's self-esteem.

Conclusion

The results of the survey have formed the basis for the remainder of our study. This chapter has merely laid the groundwork.

The next four chapters will discuss the influences Christian women feel destroy their self-esteem. We will see how these destroyers affect us and how we can work to overcome them.

Chapters six through twelve will focus on self-esteem builders. We will study how to improve our own self-esteem as well as how to build self-esteem in others.

Christian women can and should have good self-esteem. Hopefully, as you go through this study, you will grow closer to God, to your fellow Christians and to your family. As a result, you will feel better about yourself than you ever have before and be a more useful servant for God. I want you to be able to say, "I am special to God. I love me!"

For Thought & Discussion

1. Run off copies of the questionnaire and have your ladies' class complete it. Have someone compile the results and compare it with the results of the survey found in the Appendix.

2. Have some members of the class make posters comparing characteristics of women with a low self-esteem and women with a high self-esteem.

3. Allow each class member to share a specific person who has influenced their self-esteem for good.

4. Why do frequent prayer and Bible study contribute to a high self-esteem?

5. Discuss any conclusions based on the survey that may have been surprising to you.

6. Read the following scriptures and discuss how they affect the Christian's self-esteem: Genesis 1:27; Philippians 4; Ephesians 5:8-10; II Corinthians 3:4-6; Proverbs 22:1-2; I Peter 2:9-10.

7. Read Luke 10:27 and James 2:8. List some specific ways we demonstrate that we love ourselves. How does the way we love ourselves affect how we love others?

8. Discuss how self-esteem affects the different areas of a Christian's life.

PART I: SELF-ESTEEM DESTROYERS

2

Guilt, Anxiety & Fear

The next four chapters will deal with self-esteem destroyers. These are influences that most commonly cause Christian women to have poor self-esteem. We want to examine how these negative influences affect us and how we can overcome them.

When Christian women were asked what had the greatest influence in causing them to have a poor self-esteem, guilt, anxiety and fear were listed more than any other answer. One out of every four women surveyed rated these as their top answer.

Understandably, it is hard to feel good about yourself if you constantly carry the burden of guilt or if you are always worried or afraid. These are influences that hold many women back from doing the Lord's work. Let us look at them and see how we can overcome these barriers to good self-esteem.

Guilt
All of us as Christians feel guilty from time to time. We feel guilty for sins that we commit and the way our sins affect others. We also feel guilty at times because we neglect Christian responsibilities or we feel we just don't measure up to other Christians around us.

This guilt may often lead to our repentance for sin, as it makes us sorry for our sin. In this way guilt is useful. But guilt becomes a problem when we allow it to stay with us. Our mental hospitals are filled with patients who cannot deal with their guilt and go on with their lives. For many, guilt is a burden.

A Christian sister once told me that she had engaged in premarital sex. She felt so guilty about it that she believed no Christian man would ever want to marry her. Even though she had repented and God had forgiven her, she still carried the guilt.

Another Christian sister related how premarital sex made her feel guilty even after she married and how it affected her marriage. She resented her husband and felt a loss of respect for him and for herself.

Guilt affects people in different ways. It causes many people to withdraw within themselves. They want to keep their guilt feelings hidden. As a result, they don't want others to get too close to them because they are afraid someone will find out what they have done and may not like them anymore. On the other hand, others will allow their guilt to become an obsession that they talk about constantly. They continually confess their sins to others and don't allow themselves or others to forget the past.

Guilt often expresses itself in feelings of inadequacy which is a sign of low self-esteem. Some feel that because of their past they are not good enough to teach or minister to others. They want to compare themselves to other Christians. Sometimes guilt expresses itself physically. I have known people who have allowed their guilt to burden them to the point that they quit eating or they overeat. Some have turned to alcohol or drugs to ease the pain of guilt.

Perhaps the most common way guilt affects us is in our inability to accept God's forgiveness and forgive ourselves. We know the Bible says God is faithful and just to forgive, but many can't accept that and go on with their lives. As a result, they feel God is very far away.

During World War II German soldiers in concentration camps would take the bodies of dead prisoners and tie them to men who were still alive. Can you imagine walking around with a dead body tied to you? Well, that is what we do when we don't accept forgiveness and forgive ourselves. We keep carrying around the dead man of sin.

The Bible gives us many examples of people who sinned and how they dealt with their sin and guilt. In Genesis 3 we read of Adam and Eve's sin in the Garden of Eden. Notice their reaction of guilt after they sinned. Verse ten tells us they were afraid, and verses twelve and thirteen show the excuses they made for their sins.

Many Christians today follow this same pattern. I think it is especially true among our young people. When we commit sin we feel guilty and afraid. Instead of seeing God as forgiving and compassionate, we become afraid of Him and hide from Him. Instead of drawing closer to God, we grow away from God and try to make excuses that will justify our sins.

David is another biblical example of someone who sinned and had to deal with guilt. II Samuel 11 and 12 tells us of his sin with Bathsheba and Nathan's rebuke. When David realized he had sinned he responded in a completely different manner from Adam and Eve. II Samuel 12:13 is David's confession of his sin. Psalm 51 is also an expression of David's confession and a prayer for forgiveness. Rather than fearing God, he turned to God and asked for mercy and a pure heart.

We also know David prayed for the child that God said would die. Often others are affected by our sin and we must pray for them. After the child died, David washed himself and went to worship God. David did not carry the burden of guilt around with him the rest of his reign. He accepted God's forgiveness and got on with his life. We can learn much from his example.

Peter and Judas are also examples of Bible characters who handled guilt differently. Both had been with Jesus as His apostles. I often wonder what made the difference. Matthew 27:3-5 tells us that Judas was sorry for betraying Jesus. He confessed the sin and tried to correct it by returning the money, but he was so overcome by guilt that he went out and hanged himself.

Peter had promised he would never deny Jesus, but he did. The account in Luke 22:54-62 tells us Jesus turned and looked straight at Peter when the cock crowed after Peter's third denial. Imagine how guilty Peter felt. All we know, other than the fact he went out and wept bitterly, is that Peter used the rest of his life to teach others about Jesus. Apparently, he learned from his mistake and it probably made him preach more boldly and fervently about Jesus. He knew what it meant to be forgiven.

What can we learn from these examples that will help us overcome guilt? Below are six biblically-based suggestions for overcoming guilt.

1. **Stop sinning.** (Romans 6:1-2) We may carry our guilt because we have not had the courage to quit a particular sin. We must get rid of the sin before we can be free from guilt.

2. **Learn to confess sins specifically.** (I John 1:9; James 5:16) The nature of the sin usually determines whether the sin should be confessed publicly or privately. Most of our sins are of a private nature and should be confessed only to God.

Usually in our prayers we throw in "...and forgive us of our sins." Perhaps if we shared our sins specifically with God, we could feel more forgiven. For instance, "Lord, my attitude toward my friend has been harsh and critical. Please forgive me and help me to love her more."

Once you have confessed your sin, there is no need to continually keep bringing it up. God blots it out and remembers it no more.

3. **Acknowledge God's forgiveness.** (I John 1:7-9) If you have trouble accepting God's forgiveness, take time to study passages of scripture that talk about God's forgiving nature and study Bible stories in which God demonstrated His forgiveness. I think of Ahab in I Kings 21:28-29. He was such an evil king but when he humbled himself God forgave him. In your prayers, thank God for His forgiveness.

4. **Learn to forgive yourself and others.** (Matthew 6:14-15; Ephesians 4:32) We often don't forgive ourselves because we feel like others have not forgiven us. We must be careful not to add to others' guilt by not having a forgiving spirit ourselves. We often say we forgive but we hold a grudge or remind people of their past mistakes. No wonder they can't forgive themselves!

5. **Don't dwell on the past.** Learn from your mistakes and get busy with the present (Philippians 3:13-14). Paul is such a good example of this. He could have felt tremendous guilt for the way he persecuted Christians, but he said he had to forget the past. There are too many things for us to do today to waste opportunities by looking back.

6. **Think less of yourself and more about others.** (Philippians 2:3-4) When we carry the burden of guilt around we are spending too much "thought time" on ourselves. We need to replace those thoughts with more positive thoughts (Philippians 4:8) and focus our attention on others. We will be happier and we will make others happier in return.

Anxiety & Fear

I have put anxiety and fear together because fear is a form of anxiety. Both are unhealthy influences on us in a physical, spiritual and social way.

It is hard to like ourselves and have a good self-esteem when our minds are full of worry and fear. It becomes easy to dwell on negative thoughts and spend our time wondering what may happen. As a result, worry becomes a habit or a way of life. Some people would not be happy if they didn't have something to worry about. For others, life seems to be one "crisis" after another.

When we are continually anxious and fearful it is more difficult for others to like us. Have you known someone of whom you were afraid to ask, "How are you today?" You know before you ask that you will get a negative response. People tend to stay away from those rather than listen to their complaints and anxieties.

Others wear their worried looks on their faces all the time. No wonder they don't feel good about themselves when they look into the mirror and see the frown and wrinkle lines that worry and fear have placed there. They have not learned the joy that comes with a pleasant countenance.

Medical doctors have long agreed that worry and fear are the source of many illnesses and physical problems. Stomach ulcers, digestive problems, high blood pressure, and heart disease are often traced to anxiety and stress. We punish our own bodies when we worry! And then we worry because we don't feel good!

Robert Wingfied said that strengthening the body helps us handle stress. He listed the following as tips on handling stress:
• Learn to relax
• Get the proper rest
• Get regular rigorous exercise
• Eat a nutritionally balanced diet
• Lose weight
• Control all your input
• Practice good posture
• Utilize medical checkups
(via Lakewood Church of Christ Bulletin; Montgomery, Alabama)

While Mr. Wingfield gave some physical tips for handling stress, Jesus knew we need spiritual tips as well. Anxiety and fear are not new problems. Jesus saw their effects on the lives of people when He lived on earth and addressed the subject in His Sermon on the Mount (Matthew 6:25-34).

Jesus also rebuked Martha for being "careful and troubled about many things" in Luke 10:38-42. How many of us are Marthas today? It is so easy to get caught up and busy about all the little things in our lives. What will I cook? Will I get the dress made in time? Is there enough money? What will my guests think? And on and on it goes. We are so busy with all the "urgent" things in our lives that we neglect the important things. Jesus said, "Mary hath chosen the good part, which shall not be taken away from her."

maRtha's hanðs — maRy's heaRt

I must have the hands of Martha:
Hands that scrub and cook and sew—
I can have the heart of Mary
While I do these things, you know;
Though my hands are in the dishpan,
This soul of mine can soar
And in thoughts sublime and lofty
Go right up to heaven's door.

I must cook, oh endless dinners,
For dear ones have to eat;
But my soul need not be cooking—
It can sit at Jesus' feet!
Help me, God, while doing duties
Against which my soul rebels,
Meekly still to peel potatoes,
But not to grovel in the shells.

Grant me, God, 'mid things prosaic,
Ere to choose the better part;
Grant that while I must be "Martha,"
I can have a "Mary" heart.

—AUTHOR UNKNOWN

Another biblical example of anxiety and fear is Elijah. I Kings 19 tells us wicked Jezebel vowed to kill Elijah. Verses 3 and 4 say that he was afraid and ran for his life and prayed that he might die. After Elijah rested, ate and was reassured by God that there were 7,000 in Israel who had not worshipped Baal, he overcame his fear. Even a great prophet like Elijah fell prey to Satan's use of anxiety and fear for a time.

When I was a teenager I lived in constant fear of death. The thing I feared most about death was that it was inevitable. It would bother me to read I John 4:18 knowing I was so afraid of dying. As I have grown older I have realized the way to drive out the fear was to replace it with confidence—confidence of a home in heaven with God. When we are sure we have obeyed God and we will go to heaven, we don't have to be afraid of dying any more.

Jesus commanded Christians not to worry (Matthew 6:25-34), yet it is one of the most frequently broken commands. Through His word He tells us how we can overcome our anxieties and fears.

1. **Seek first His kingdom and his righteousness.** (Matthew 6:33) Jesus was teaching us to keep our priorities in order. If we are seeking the kingdom first we will eliminate many of the little things that weigh us down and cause us to worry.

2. **Stay close to God's Word.** (II Timothy 2:15) We will say this over and over in our study! There is no substitude for studying the Bible. As we study, our faith in God grows. There is no greater cure for worry and fear than a strong faith in God. I've often wondered if worry could be the opposite of faith. There is no "instant faith." Paul reminds us, "Faith comes from hearing and hearing by the Word of God" (Romans 10:17).

3. **Pray about your anxieties and fears.** (Philippians 4:6; I Peter 5:7) God told us to cast all our cares upon Him. He not only *wants* to hear them, but He can do something about them. If we pray about our problems and get up from our prayers worried and nervous, then we haven't prayed in faith (James 1:6-8). When we pray in confidence we should feel our burdens have been lifted. God will carry them for us.

What a friend we have in Jesus
All our sins and griefs to bear,
*What a **privilege** to carry*
***Everything** to God in prayer.*

4. Count your blessings. (I Thessalonians 5:18) How many times have we heard this? But it is often hard to practice. Sometimes, we as Christians need to remind each other of all our blessings. The bad things in life never look quite as bad if we stop to look at all the good.

5. Accept yourself as you are. We worry too much about ourselves. We complain because we are too short or too tall, too fat or too thin, or our nose is too big. Jesus asked, "Which of you by taking thought can add one cubit to his stature?" (Matthew 6:27) Worrying about what we do not have, whether physical beauty, material possessions or talents, will not give us more.

If there is something about ourselves that we can change and improve, then we should do it. It may mean disciplining ourselves to lose weight or getting a more flattering hair style. Rather than worry about something over which we have no control, we must accept it and be content.

An acceptance of self enables us to be ourselves, and that is a prerequisite to peace of mind and good self esteem.

The world is wide
In time and tide,
And God is guide,
Then—do not hurry.

That man is blest
Who does his best
And leaves the rest
Then—do not worry.
—CHARLES F. DEEMS

Conclusion

Every Christian's self-esteem has probably been affected by guilt, fear or anxiety at some point in his life. Guilt, fear and anxiety destroy self-esteem because they focus our attention on ourselves rather than on God. They cause us not to depend on God. They also affect our self-esteem by their physical effects on our bodies. It is hard to feel good about ourselves when we physically feel bad. This is especially true when we have inflicted the physical burdens on ourselves.

If guilt, anxiety and fear have caused you to have a poor self-esteem, then take steps to overcome them. These are problems between you and God, and He provides the solutions to the problems. You can improve your self-esteem!

For Thought & Discussion

▦ 1. Share some things you have feared and how you conquered that fear.

▦ 2. Find other examples of Bible characters who experienced guilt, anxiety or fear and discuss how it affected them.

▦ 3. Discuss some ways we can help others who bear the burden of guilt and worry.

▦ 4. Have someone do some medical research on how guilt, anxiety and fear can affect us physically.

▦ 5. Use a concordance and other Bible reference materials to find scriptures that talk about God's forgiving nature. Have class members share some scriptures they study when they are afraid or worried.

▦ 6. Discuss ways in which our sins affect others. How does our guilt, anxiety and fear affect others?

▦ 7. Make a list of the things you are worried about or afraid of. Beside it, list your blessings.

3

Criticism & Lack of Encouragement

In the last chapter we discussed what Christian women considered to be the greatest influence causing them to have a poor self-esteem. That influence was guilt, anxiety and fear. According to the survey, almost as many women considered criticism and lack of encouragement to be the greatest influence toward poor self-esteem. One out of every five women surveyed listed criticism and lack of encouragement as their first choice.

Obviously, criticism can affect our self-esteem. It is probably the most direct attack on our self-esteem because it is inflicted by others. It can cause wounds that hurt deeply and result either in withdrawal or in anger and resentment. Criticism can cause us to think less of ourselves, and it destroys our self-confidence because we feel that others don't think highly of us.

Imagine what it would be like to live in a home where your husband was always critical. (Five percent of those surveyed said their husbands had contributed to their poor self-esteem.) How would you feel about yourself if he continually criticized your appearance, your cooking, your housekeeping skills, your ability as a mother, or the way you manage your time? Or what if your husband always compared you with other women and asked, "Why can't you be like Bob's wife? She's always..." Is it any wonder that women who live in a situation like this may have a low self-esteem? Other women cry out, "My husband doesn't appreciate me. He takes me for granted." Perhaps these women do not have critical husbands, but their husbands offer no encouragement or praise. As a result, the wife's self-esteem suffers.

Often people come to church to get away from situations such as this. They feel church is the one place where they can find encouragement and love and escape from criticism. How sad it is that many times critical attitudes also creep into the church, even though we are warned against it (Philippians 2:14). One who comes to church hoping to find encouragement may come only to learn that a Christian sister has been critical behind her back or she may leave still feeling a void because no one offered any personal encouragement. (We will devote an entire chapter (Chapter 10) to discussing the importance of praise and encouragement. It is one of the greatest influences we can have in helping Christians build a good self-esteem.)

We need to be reminded time and time again of Ephesians 4:29; 31-32 which says, "Do not let any unwholesome talk come out of your mouths, but only what is good for *building others up according to their needs*, that it may benefit those who listen. Get rid of all bitterness, rage and anger, brawling and slander, along with every form of malice. Be kind and compassionate to one another, forgiving each other, just as in Christ God forgave you."

We are all attacked by criticism. It seems no one can escape it forever. Criticism is not a new problem. We read of it beginning with Cain and Abel (Genesis 4) and continue to find examples throughout the Bible. Even Paul and Barnabas were critical of one another and went their separate ways (Acts 15:39,40). Perhaps the greatest example of criticism is the nation of Israel. Time and time again they became critical and murmured. It seemed they would never learn. Even Jesus was criticized for healing on the Sabbath, eating with sinners, and allowing the woman to annoint Him with expensive perfume.

Often those who are in positions of leadership receive the most criticism and the least amount of encouragement. How many times have we heard our elders, deacons, preachers and Bible class teachers criticized? Too many times we want to name all the things they do that are wrong or that we don't agree with, yet we seldom offer them words, notes, or cards of thanks for the many things they do right. When we find ourselves becoming critical of our church leaders, we need to read passages such as Hebrews 13:17 and I Thessalonians 5:12-13. These scriptures tell us to respect and obey those who are over us and hold them in highest regard.

Types of Criticism

Webster's dictionary uses four definitions to describe criticism: (1) to evaluate, (2) to stress the faults, (3) to complain and (4) to judge.

Only one of those definitions, *to evaluate,* can have a positive effect on one's self-esteem. At times we may ask others to give us their opinion or help us evaluate an area of our lives. If done in a spirit of love this can be beneficial. It is called "constructive criticism."

I have received much constructive criticism in writing this book. People edited and offered suggestions for improvement. Parents may give their children constructive criticism. Can't you just hear a mother saying, "I really like that sweater, but I don't think it matches your pants." We must be careful to give our evaluations in a positive manner.

On the other hand, the three remaining types of criticism are negative and scriptures warn us not to participate in them. If we consider others better than ourselves (Philippians 2:3-4) we will not continually stress their faults. Philippians 2:14 tells us to do everything without complaining or arguing, and Matthew 7:1-2 commands us not to judge others. If we are the type of people who complain, judge, and stress others' faults, we are affecting their self-esteem. I would hate to think someone had a poor self-esteem because of my critical attitude. Not only that, but the complainers and criticizers cause others not to like them. People do not enjoy being around those who are always criticizing, complaining, or judging.

Why People Criticize

When we hear others being critical or find ourselves having critical attitudes, we may need to ask why. Is the criticism justifiable or profitable or will it cause damage? Note the following list of reasons for criticizing:

1. Many times the chronic fault-finder criticizes because she has a poor image of herself. She feels that she can boost her own self-esteem by making others look bad. Pulling others down makes her feel important. This is often the case in a situation where a woman receives no praise or encouragement from others. Since no one else will praise her, she praises herself by criticizing others. In most cases, she is only deceiving herself.

2. Others may criticize because they have a self-righteous attitude. They feel that because they have been a Christian longer or appear to be more involved in the Lord's work, they have a "right" to judge others. We never see this attitude in Jesus and He was the most righteous man who ever lived. Jesus Himself criticized the Pharisees because of their self-righteous attitudes (Matthew 23). We must realize when we point our finger in judgment of others there are three fingers pointing back at us.

a thought for today

Don't find fault with the man who limps
Or stumbles along life's road,
Unless you have worn the shoes he wears,
Or struggled beneath his load.
There may be tacks in his shoes that hurt,
Though hidden away from our view.

The burden he bears, if placed on your back
Might cause you to stumble, too.
Don't be too hard on the man who errs,
Or pelt him with wood or stone,
Unless you are sure—yea, double sure,
That you have no fault of your own.
—CENTRAL CHURCH OF CHRIST BULLETIN, NORFOLK, VA

3. Another reason people may criticize is because they are jealous or hold a grudge against the one they criticize. We often criticize those who disagree with us, even though it may only be a matter of opinion. If this is the problem, instead of criticizing, we should go to that person, settle the matter, ask for forgiveness and then go on. That is what Jesus taught in Matthew 5:23-24. Being critical only causes jealousy, grudges, and hard feelings to grow and fester.

4. A fourth reason people criticize is habit. Many criticize or complain without thinking. They haven't learned when to be silent. Proverbs 11:12 says, "A man who lacks judgment derides his neighbor, but a man of understanding holds his tongue." I kept James 1:19 taped to my refrigerator door for months to remind myself not to talk too much. It says, "Everyone should be quick to listen, slow to speak, and slow to become angry."

Two Christian brothers were studying Philippians 2:14, "Do everything without complaining," and decided to see if they were complainers. They challenged each other to count the number of times they complained during the next week. One brother said he quit counting after 75 times. He had learned a lesson. Complaining and criticizing is habit forming and he had to break the habit.

Overcoming Critical Attitudes
Since our criticism directly affects others' self-esteem we should make every effort to overcome critical attitudes. Below are some suggestions that could help.

1. **Learn to think positively.** "As a man thinketh in his heart, so is he." Our verbal criticism begins with critical thoughts. We must discipline our thoughts before we can discipline our tongue. Philippians 4:8 reminds us to think about things that are true, noble, right, pure, lovely, and admirable. When we find ourselves beginning to criticize, we should stop and think about the good in that person.

Research has shown children usually live up to their teacher's expectations. If a teacher labels a child as a troublemaker, he probably will be. Another teacher may expect the same child to be well-behaved. In her class there is no discipline problem with the child. Could the same be true in the church? If there were less criticism and more positive expressions in our thoughts and comments to others, we might be surprised how much more loving and caring the church would become.

2. **Learn to be quiet.** My mother used to always say, "If you can't say anything good, don't say anything." (Aren't mothers wise?) Solomon wrote, "When words are many, sin is not absent, but he who holds his tongue is wise" (Proverbs 10:19). It is better not to say anything than to say something that will hurt someone. Jesus taught that we will have to give account for every idle word we say (Matthew 12:36-37). What greater lesson could we have on the importance of silence?

Being quiet also means not talking behind someone's back. We rarely criticize someone to his face. Criticism hurts even more deeply when you learn someone has been critical of you to others. We offer so many apologies because of things we have said that would have been better left unsaid. Ecclesiastes 10:20 warns us to watch what we say even in our bedrooms, "because a bird of the air may carry your words, and a bird on the wing may report what you say."

3. **Before criticizing, learn all the facts.** It is easy to jump to conclusions and judge people only on what we see. A preacher once said, "I never criticize church members' giving. I don't know if they are supporting elderly parents or have other worthwhile uses for their money."

If we will take the time to get to know people better we may learn our criticisms were wrong. We may become much more compassionate and understanding of that person and find ways to help him.

4. **Be careful how you say things.** It is not just what we say that is important but *how* we say it. Our tone of voice, inflections, and facial expressions may say more than our words do. Wise Solomon wrote, "A soft answer turns away wrath, but grievous words stir up anger" (Proverbs 15:1).

We may not say anything critical, but our sarcasm and joking may still convey a critical message to others. Some people do not have to say anything because their faces say it all. "You can read her like a book," some say. It all goes back to what is in our hearts.

5. **Evaluate your criticism.** Before expressing critical feelings to others, ask yourself some questions. Is my criticism just? Have I learned all the facts? Could my criticism be beneficial? If the answers are yes, then go to the person you are critical of. We spend too much time criticizing people behind their backs because we lack the courage to go to them personally. We never see this in Jesus. He taught us to go and talk to our brother or sister privately (Matthew 18:15).

When You Are Criticized

Criticism is a two-way street. We can be the criticizers and attack others' self-esteem or we may find ourselves being criticized. In the second case, it is our self-esteem that is being attacked or destroyed. Criticism hurts and it is only natural to feel pain when you are criticized. Some allow criticism to dampen their enthusiasm. Those who plan any church event such as a luncheon, ladies-seminar, or retreat learn quickly that they can't please everyone. When some are criticized they quickly want to give up or say, "Well, why doesn't she do it if she has all the answers?" Some even allow criticism to cause resentment toward the one who criticized and may criticize them in return.

How should Christians act when we are criticized? Jane McWhorter, in her book *Let This Cup Pass*, devoted an entire chapter to unjust criticism. In that chapter, she lists seven ways to handle unjust criticism. Mrs. McWhorter's suggestions are:

1. **Be rational.** It is important to examine the criticism honestly and see if there is a need to make a change. We must not over-react or react without praying and thinking about what has been said. If the criticism is unjust, then it may be best to forget about it.

2. **Act instead of reacting.** Rather than reacting on our instincts we must learn to be the master of the situation and plan our actions (Proverbs 14:22). Don't allow others to decide how you are going to act.

3. **Bite your tongue.** When we are hurt by someone, the natural instinct is to lash back; but it takes a big person to walk away from a fight. We should allow time to elapse before speaking (Proberbs 29:11). It is so easy to say something we will later regret. We must be mature enough not to become offended too easily.

4. **Learn to forgive.** Anyone can love those who are nice to him but loving those who have wronged him is often a different matter. Sometimes we feel we have been hurt too deeply to forgive, but we still must forgive just as Christ did (Colossians 3:13). We forgive others, not for what they are, but for what we are. If we feel we simply cannot forgive, then pray, "Father, I want to forgive but I can't. Please help me."

5. **Smother your critic with kindness.** Rather than lashing back with unkind words or actions, try going out of your way to be nice to the person who has mistreated you. Kindness makes it extremely dificult for the offender to continue his attacks (Romans 12:14-20). Be sincere in your kindness. Kindness shown without love will be hypocritical and may only cause more hurt.

6. **Should the matter be discussed?** Frequently it is best to sit down and discuss the matter with the offender. However, before this takes place a person should allow a "cooling off" time to elapse in which she can think about the matter, understand both her reactions and the motives of the critics, search God's Word, and pray over the matter. Sometimes it is wise just to let the matter drop. Talk it over with God and do what you think is expedient.

7. **Try sublimation.** Instead of working off frustrations with attacks against the critic or against innocent people, it would be better to throw one's energies into an unrelated situation. Do something to further the kingdom of God and help others and leave the rest to God.

Conclusion

If criticism has caused you to have a poor self-esteem, then perhaps following these seven suggestions will help you feel better about yourself. We will never be free from criticism, but if we can learn how to handle others' criticisms and not become critical ourselves then our self-esteem will be under God's control rather than our own.

If your self-esteem suffers because you are constantly criticized at home by your husband or children, then sit down with them and explain your feelings. Use this time to discuss ways each family member can offer more encouragement to one another. Pray about it together.

Criticism hurts! It is a direct attack on one's self-esteem. With God's help, we can learn to deal with it and not allow it to destroy our self-esteem.

For Thought & Discussion

▓ 1. Ask each member of the class to share a verse from Proverbs that talks about the tongue. You may wish to illustrate some of these verses on posters for your classroom. Discuss how these verses can affect self-esteem.

▓ 2. How are Christians to react when we hear others being critical or complaining? Role-play some different responses we could offer.

▓ 3. Discuss the effects of criticism on the church and your congregation's leaders. How does this affect our outreach in the community?

▓ 4. Think of someone whose self-esteem may be suffering from a lack of encouragement. Stop now and write them a note of encouragement. (We'll discuss this more in Chapter 10.)

▓ 5. Memorize Philippians 2:14. Say it together as a class.

▓ 6. Why do some people allow criticism to hurt their self-esteem more than others. What are some coping strategies to use when we are criticized?

4

The World's Values

"Love not the world, neither the things that are in the world. If any man loves the world, the love of the Father is not in him. For all that is in the world, the lust of the flesh, and the lust of the eyes, and the pride of life, is not of the Father, but is of the world. And the world passeth away, and the lust thereof: but he that doeth the will of God abideth forever" (I John 2:15-17, KJV).

How many times have we read that passage and heard sermons on it? Many of us know it and can quote it, yet our hearts do not really know the meaning.

It is easy to say, "Love not the world...," but Satan has made the world so appealing. Satan has made the things that are worldly appear to be very beautiful to tempt us. Just notice the advertisements on television. Advertisers use handsome men and beautiful women to sell their wine and beer. They are surrounded by beautiful scenery and a lot of friends and fun. Would people be tempted to drink nearly as much if the advertisers showed the "gutters" with their drunks or homes that are torn apart by what alcohol has done?

Satan will do his best to make us want to love the world and he uses a variety of sources. He makes us afraid to be different from the world even though God tells us not to be conformed to the pattern of this world (Romans 12:2). When Satan makes us feel embarrassed because we are different from the world in the manner we think and live and dress and talk, he has succeeded in attacking our self-esteem. Satan wants the world to determine how we feel about ourselves rather than God.

How is Satan doing? Sixteen percent of the Christian women surveyed said the world's values influenced them to have a poor self-esteem. We see Satan's efforts even more when we notice the answers given to the question of which influences contribute most to having a poor self-esteem. The top answers were non-Christian friends (34%), the media (21%), and associates at work or school (20%). Satan uses our peers, associates, and the media to try to make us think less of ourselves.

Peer pressure especially attacks our young people. The desire to be accepted and popular is very strong among teenagers. When non-Christian friends begin to ask, "Why don't you dance?" or "Why do you want to stay pure?" or when there is pressure to drink, curse, take drugs, etc., the Christian feels his self-esteem is on the line. He feels if he does not participate, he will not be accepted, but if he does participate he knows it is wrong and bears the guilt of sin.

Adults often experience the same type of pressure on the job. They hear their associates discussing the "fun parties" and who can drink the most. They laugh and joke and turn to the Christian and say, "It's a pity you church-goers never have any fun," or "What do you do for a good time, Christian?" Once again, our self-esteem is under fire.

Perhaps Satan is waging one of his biggest battles for our self-esteem with the media. Magazines, newspapers and television are constantly keeping the world's values before us. The feminist movement has made sure to get its fair share of media attention to make us aware of what a "real woman" of today is supposed to be like. Talk shows often encourage the "anything goes" attitude on moral issues and make light of religion.

After I quit working, I would often watch the Phil Donahue Show in the mornings. It was an eye-opening experience for me. I began to realize just how different Christians are. I never realized how American women feel about many controversial issues, but it became apparent to me that we have a real war with Satan on our hands. Now, more than ever, we must take a stand and be bold about what we believe. We have been silent too long.

What are the values of the world? They are no different today than when the Bible was written. We read earlier in I John 2:17 that the things of the world are the lust of the flesh, the lust of the eyes, and the pride of life. Let us examine each one separately.

The Lust Of The Flesh

The New International Version refers to the lust of the flesh as the cravings of sinful man. That can include many things, but I think Satan often disguises these cravings and calls them pleasure.

The world today seems to live for pleasure, and it seeks out pleasure in many different ways. Some seek pleasure in sexual affairs, some in alcoholic beverages, some in drugs, some in gambling, and on and on. The Christian may not be tempted by these pleasures as much as pleasures which are not sinful in themselves, but they take priority over God's work. For instance, we may take a weekend trip to an amusement park and miss church services on Sunday in order to travel. There is nothing sinful about the trip itself, but it becomes sinful if it interferes with our commitment to God. We must be very careful that our desire to have a good time does not take priority over our desire to serve God.

Jesus referred to this in the parable of the sower (Luke 8:4-15). He taught the thorny soil was those who heard the word, but were choked out by life's worries, riches, and pleasure (verse 14). He said they do not mature. Could it be we have Christians today who allow pleasure to keep them from growing and maturing in Christ?

Paul wrote to Timothy and gave instructions regarding widows. He compared two types of widows in I Timothy 5:5-6: "The widow who is really in need and left all alone puts her hope in God and continues night and day to pray and to ask God for help. But the widow who *lives for pleasure* is dead even while she lives." This can apply to all. We are to seek God first rather than pleasure. Solomon taught this in Ecclesiastes. Read Ecclesiastes 2:1-3 and find that even after he "refused his heart no pleasure" (2:10) he found pleasure vanity or meaningless. His conclusion was to fear God and keep His commandments (Ecclesiastes 12:13).

This is not to say Christians cannot enjoy pleasurable activities and be happy. Certainly, if the activities are not in conflict with God's law or do not interfere with our commitment, there is nothing wrong. But we must be careful not to live for pleasure as the world seems to do.

Pleasure is not to be confused with happiness. Happiness comes from within and pleasure from without. Bars are filled with laughing, smiling people who are searching for happiness through pleasure. Behind the laughs and smiles most are lonely. They have failed to realize that true happiness comes from a right relationship with God. That's why Christians can be the happiest people on earth in addition to having the highest self-esteem.

Lust Of The Eyes

People of the world often base their opinions of others on what they see. They notice what we wear, the car (or cars) we drive, where we live and how we spend our money. Everyone is working hard to "keep up with the Joneses" in order to make a good impression. This, in turn, supposedly boosts our self-esteem. In short, the world values materialism. Many feel like "what others have, I need also." "Necessities" now include owning your home, driving two nice cars, a color television with recorder and video games, a microwave oven, and at least two new outfits each season. If we don't have these "essentials" we sometimes feel inferior, and there goes our self-esteem.

As a result, many women have left their homes and gone to work in order to have these material possessions. We don't like to feel inferior. I realize with today's economy that many women must work and their families depend on their income. On the other hand, other women work to provide their families with more material possessions. I am not saying it is wrong for Christian women to work outside the home. Once again, it is a matter of priority. We must be on guard against allowing material possessions to become our goal. Young children need their mother's care and attention much more than they need a big house, a color television or toys.

Once we are caught up in materialism, we never seem to be content. We always want more. Solomon wrote, "Whoever loves money never has money enough; whoever loves wealth is never satisfied with his income. This, too, is meaningless" (Ecclesiastes 5:10).

Paul wrote about contentment in I Timothy 6:6-10. Take time to study the passage prayerfully. He said materialism leads us into temptation and can cause us to leave the faith. Paul said to be content if you have food and clothing. (He didn't even include owning your own house!) We need to sit and look at what we have without comparing ourselves to others. As long as we compare, we will always come up wanting something else. We are all rich indeed and should spend more time thanking God rather than wanting more. Our self-esteem should be based on what we have, but it should be based on what we have *spiritually* rather than materially. We should never feel inferior when we stop to count our spiritual blessings.

The Pride Of Life

Satan's most vicious attack on the self-esteem of American women has come through his attack on our pride. What does the pride of life involve? The New International Version renders this phrase as "the boasting of what he has and what he does." In recent years Satan has used the feminist movement and the fight for ERA to cause women to want to boast.

How does Satan attack our pride? His first attack is on the self-esteem of housewives and mothers. Housewives have been made to feel unworthy of recognition, unappreciated and a little stupid for wanting to stay home and raise a family. Comments such as "Don't you get bored?" or "I would go crazy if I stayed home all day" are some darts Satan throws at the housewives' self-esteem.

Guests on the Phil Donahue Show one morning included a female doctor, lawyer and accountant. All three had left their professions to become full-time mothers. These women expressed complete satisfaction, but many in the audience attacked their decision to leave a career. On numerous occasions I've heard Donahue ask housewives if all they do is read magazines, bake cookies, and watch soap operas. He goes on to ask, "How do you find any fulfillment for yourself in staying home?"

Many cannot understand that being a housewife and mother can be the most fulfilling job of all. Its reward may not come in money, promotions, or the praise of others, but it has many rewards. Much of the fulfillment is based on our attitudes.

I'm a housewife

My days are days of small affairs, of trifling worries, little cares.
A lunch to pack, a bed to make, a room to sweep, a pie to bake.
A hurt to kiss, a tear to dry, a head to brush, a bow to tie.
A face to wash, a rent to mend, a meal to plan, a fuss to end.
A sleepy child to be put to bed, a hungry husband to be fed.
I, who had hoped someday to gain Success, perhaps a bit of fame.
I just give my life to small affairs, to trifling worries, little cares.
But should tomorrow bring a change,
my little house grow still and strange—
Should all the cares I know today be swept quite suddenly away—
Where now a hundred duties press, would be an ache of loneliness...
No child's gay ribbon to be tied, no wayward little feet to guide.
To heaven then would rise my prayers;
"God, give me back my little cares."
How thankful I should ever be, to be where God intended me.
                                                    —AUTHOR UNKNOWN

Even with today's attacks on housewives' self-esteem, our survey indicated there is almost no difference in the self-esteem of the Christian housewife and working woman. Thirty-nine percent of both groups rated their self-esteem in the very high range. Perhaps this indicates Christian women recognize their place at home is God-given, and they refuse to let the world convince them it is an unworthy job.

Satan's second attack on our pride is selfishness. He is trying his best to take our minds off our husbands, children, and the church and focus our attention on ourselves. He appeals to our pride by making us think, "What do others think of me?" or "How can I put more excitement and fulfillment in *my* life?" Once again, Satan attacks our self-esteem.

Women today are encouraged to get an education, pursue an exciting career, be aggressive and seek their highet level of potential. Let me quickly state, there is nothing wrong with these things in and of themselves. We must be careful, however, and ask ourselves *why* we are seeking them. Are we working outside the home merely to "keep up with the Joneses" and gain the material possessions we desire? Do we seek a promotion in order to receive the praise of others? Do we seek fulfillment outside the home in order to have something to boast about and make us feel important?

Jesus condemned the Pharisees in John **12:43**, saying "they loved the praise of men more than the praise of God." We must not allow Satan to tempt us to seek man's approval before God's. That is the "pride of life." Again, let me say there is nothing wrong with working outside the home or seeking fulfillment of our needs. The Bible gives us examples of women who did (Lydia, Priscilla, and the virtuous woman of Proverbs 31). We must not, however, become so caught up in our own individual jobs or whatever we do to find fulfillment that we neglect the needs of others. This is when Satan turns our pride into selfishness.

Having a good self-esteem does not mean being the center of attention or seeking our own needs to the exclusion of others' needs. A good self-esteem usually goes hand-in-hand with unselfishness. The highest form of fulfillment comes from unselfishly giving yourself away. Philippians 2:3-4 teaches this principle when it says, "Do nothing out of selfish ambition or vain conceit, but in humility consider others better than yourselves. Each of you should look not only to your own interests, but also to the interests of others."

The opposite of pride is humility. Pride focuses attention on ourselves. Humility focuses attention on others.

Conclusion

Satan is ever present. He is always searching for new ways to tempt us that the world's values are better than God's. Christ did not escape this temptation (Matthew 4) yet what a comfort it is to know He remained without sin (Hebrews 4:15). If we keep our eyes focused upon God's word, Satan's power will lose its beautiful appeal.

Even though the world's values may influence our self-esteem and try to make us feel inferior, Christians must never give in. Jesus has called us away from worldly things. He said, "If you belonged to the world, it would love you as its own. As it is, you do not belong to the world, but I have chosen you out of the world." (John 15:19).

What greater boost could our self-esteem have than to know that Jesus has chosen us and set us apart? Christians are special people!

For Thought & Discussion

▓ 1. Make a list of some specific ways Christians are different from the world. Discuss how being different affects your self-esteem and how others feel toward you.

▓ 2. Bring in magazine articles and newspaper clippings that show how the media reinforces the world's values. Discuss how Christians should react to the media's attack on Christian principles.

▓ 3. What are some pleasurable activities our young people can participate in? How can we encourage them to stay away from worldly things?

▓ 4. Compare our reactions to visitors at church who are rich and those who are poor. How do we influence their self-esteem?

▓ 5. Discuss some specific fulfilling rewards that come from 1) being a housewife and mother; and 2) from working outside the home.

▓ 6. Try to think of other worldly values that were not discussed in this chapter and discuss them in class.

▓ 7. Read Matthew 16:24-26. Discuss how this passage relates to the values of the world.

▓ 8. Contrast the Christian woman's attitude toward her job with that of women in the world. What are some things that influence whether a Christian woman should or should not work outside the home?

5

Your Appearance

In the last three chapters we have discussed the three greatest influences that Christian women feel cause them to have a poor self-esteem. According to our survey, the fourth most listed influence was early family background; however, since it was listed more frequently as an influence toward a good self-esteem, we will study its importance in a later chapter.

The influence that ranked fifth in causing a poor self-esteem was personal appearance. Nine percent of those participating in the survey said their appearances hindered their self-esteem. Many women wrote in specific comments about their appearance such as, "I've always been self-conscious about my crooked teeth," "I gained thirty pounds last year," "I'm too tall," "I'm overweight," and "My age has affected my appearance."

It is interesting to note that in our survey results, appearance and beauty ranked last among the eight influences that cause a good self-esteem. Obviously, to the Christian woman being beautiful does not mean everything or guarantee a good self-esteem, but a poor appearance certainly can cause a low self-esteem.

Should Christians be concerned about their appearance? Is it important? Dr. James Dobson wrote *Hide Or Seek* to help parents build self-esteem in children. He says, "Without question, the most highly valued personal attribute in our culture (and most others) is physical attractiveness." He goes on to say, "Most of the major choices made by adults are influenced in one way or another by the attribute of beauty." Certainly, this goes along with what the Lord told Samuel in I Samuel 16:7, "The Lord does not look at the things man looks at... **Man looks at the outward appearance**, but the Lord looks at the heart."

It is no secret that people of the world place great importance on our outward appearance. One just has to sit back and notice the contrast in the responses a beautiful woman receives from those an unattractive woman receives. Men consider appearance to be important. Dr. Dobson writes, "Most men attempt to 'capture' a mate with the greatest possible beauty. A very attractive spouse is a highly desirable prize to be displayed." Dr. Dobson goes on to comment about how appearance affects the working woman:

> Research shows that at least half of the working women who get a face lift can expect to receive salary increases in the months that follow. It is clear that beauty is a highly marketable commodity in the business world. Most bosses seek attractive secretaries and receptionists, whereas homely women often find it difficult to obtain a job of any kind.

What has brought about this tremendous emphasis on beauty? Dr. Dobson believes it is a by-product of the sexual revolution going on around us. He adds, "The more steamed up a culture becomes over sex, the more it will reward beauty and punish ugliness." Perhaps another cause is television. Women are constantly exposed to beautiful women on television. Advertising does its part on television to tempt us with hundreds of cosmetics, soaps, creams, shampoos, diet-aids, and clothes to help us become more beautiful.

How does all this affect the Christian woman? We know God looks at our hearts and not our appearance. We are told to regard no one from a worldly point of view (II Corinthians 5:16). Does this mean Christians should not be concerned with their outward appearance? Can we ignore how the people we work with, live around, and meet daily view us? Is it wrong to be beautiful?

37

I personally believe we cannot neglect our personal appearance. It affects the way others feel about us, and it also affects the way we feel about ourselves. I also believe our outward beauy should be a reflection of the beauty within our hearts. That inward beauty cannot be bought in a store or judged in a contest, but it can be seen.

I once knew a girl who married a very attractive man. I could not understand how they ever got together because he was so handsome and she was much less than beautiful. Everyone knew he could have had his pick of pretty girls. I often wondered what he saw in her. With the passing of time I was able to get to know this girl better. The more I got to know her, the more I realized her husband had married her for her inward beauty. She was so unselfish and kind and worked so hard. As I got to know her, she seemed less and less unattractive.

This is an example of what God meant in I Peter 3:3-6. Read it now and examine your life. Do people consider you beautiful because of your natural beauty or your clothes or are you beautiful because of your inner self?

It is not wrong to have natural beauty or expensive clothing. Lucky you if you do! The Bible gives us examples of beautiful women. Sarah's beauty caused Abraham to lie about their relationship (Genesis 12:11). Isaac's wife, Rebekah, is described as being very beautiful (Genesis 24:16). When Jacob stayed with Laban he noticed Leah had weak eyes, but Rachel was lovely in form and beautiful (Genesis 29:16). The virtuous woman of Proverbs 31 was clothed in fine linen and purple. Wasn't Esther lucky? Not only was she blessed with natural beauty, but she received twelve months of beauty treatments in King Xerxes' harem (Esther 2:9,21)! She used her beauty to save God's people.

God never condemns being beautiful, but he did give Christian women some advice. Paul wrote Timothy and told him to instruct the women "...to dress modestly, with decency and propriety, not with braided hair or gold or pearls or expensive clothes, but with good deeds, appropriate for women who profess to worship God" (I Timothy 2:9-10). God never wants a woman's outside appearance to outshine what is on the inside.

An expensive wardrobe, lots of make-up, and the latest hair style will never cover up a heart that is not right with God. It is only a camouflage for the world to see. We must be careful not to place too much importance on outward beauty. Real beauty begins on the inside. How many mothers have told their daughters, "Pretty is as pretty does." We must never spend so much time making our outside pretty that our inside goes unattended.

What can the Christian woman do if her self-esteem is affected by her appearance? Some women are so self-conscious about their appearance that they literally withdraw. If that is the case, perhaps the suggestions listed below can help.

Suggestions For Improving Appearance

1. **Work on your inward appearance.** I have tried to stress throughout this chapter that the Christian's beauty comes from within and radiates outward. Reread I Peter 3:1-3 and I Timothy 2:9-10 where God talks about the unfading beauty of the inner self.

Perhaps we need to add more prayer and Bible study to our inward wardrobe. The fruits of the Spirit (love, joy, peace, patience, kindness, goodness, faithfulness, gentleness and self-control) are all essentials to our inward beauty. When our thoughts are good it is much easier to wear a smile on our faces, and every woman is more beautiful when she smiles.

Before going on with any of the other suggestions, examine your inner self. How is it being reflected to others? That is where we must begin our work. When the inside is right, it will make a difference in our outward appearance.

2. **Take a good long look in a full-length mirror.** Sometime when you are alone look in the mirror and decide what your good physical features are and where you need work. Write them down. Don't be bashful about writing down your physical features that are good. These are your "assets" and you will use them to build on. Every woman has some beautiful features. If you do not believe that you do, ask your husband. He may think you are the most beautiful woman in the world. If you are single, ask your parents. No parents think their child is ugly and they can point out your assets.

After you list your assets, list your "defects," or areas you feel need work. Go from head to toe. Consider such things as your hair, your make-up, the shape of your face, your posture, your figure, your weight, your smile, how you sit, stand, and walk, and your overall physical condition. This is your personal list and you don't have to show it to anyone. Use it as a starting point to work on your outward appearance. Make the most of your assets and work on the other areas.

3. **Seek advice from others.** After you have pinpointed your assets and listed the areas of your appearance that need some work, seek the advice of someone who can help you.

If your problem is weight, go to your doctor and allow him to prescribe a diet and exercise program. Many women who are overweight have a low self-esteem because of their weight. If that is your case, do something about it! You can change your weight, but do it with a doctor's supervision. Many of today's fad diets do not contain important nutrients and can lead to other medical problems.

If you want to work on your hair, go to a good hair stylist and allow them to work with the shape of your face, quality and texture of your hair to find the hair style that is best suited to you. A new flattering hair style can often be a big boost to a woman's self-esteem.

Does your make-up need work? There are many cosmetics consultants who give free facials and offer advice on wearing make-up. Often a few little tips can add a glow to one's face. The Christian woman should not want to overdo her cosmetics, but that touch of blush and eye shadow can sometimes make a big difference in a woman's appearance and her confidence.

Perhaps your wardrobe needs work, but you don't have the money to buy a lot of new clothes. First of all, go through your closet and mend any rips, tears, or hems that need changing. Get rid of or give away clothes you never wear anymore. Then ask a friend whose manner of dress you admire to come make some suggestions. Often a new blouse, piece of jewelry or scarf can make an old outfit look like new. Find out what colors you wear best and keep that in mind when shopping for new clothes. There are many books available to help you find your best color and style.

You can spend a lot of money improving your appearance, but you don't have to. Always remember your assets and make the most of them. The cosmetics, hair style and wardrobe can be added to or worked on gradually.

4. **Take care of your body.** A beautiful face cannot hide long behind an unhealthy body. Paul told the Corinthians that our body is the temple of the Holy Spirit and we are to honor God with our body (I Corinthians 6:19-20). He later told them to purify themselves from everything that contaminates body and spirit (II Corinthians 7:1).

God gave us our bodies as a temporary house for our soul, and He expects us to take care of that house. That involves not abusing our bodies with cigarettes, alcohol, drugs, excessive weight, or over-exhaustion. It also involves eating properly and getting plenty of rest and exercise.

Our doctors' offices would be far less crowded if we would practice good health habits. We must practice the things that keep us well and abstain from those things that harm our bodies. Good health habits can add extra energy and vitality as well as put a glow in our cheeks and a sparkle in our eyes.

5. **Work on your appearance early in the day.** This is easy for the working woman who must dress and get off to her job. It is often more difficult for the woman who stays at home, particularly the woman with small children. She is busy getting her husband's shirt ironed, the children dressed, and breakfast cooked. Then there are clothes to wash, beds to make, and countless other distractions. Halfway through the morning, the doorbell rings and the woman finds herself apologizing for her appearance. She had helped everyone in her family look nice but herself. Sound familiar? Apologizing for the way you look does not do much to build your self-esteem.

Anne Ortlund, in her book *Disciplines Of The Beautiful Woman*, recommends that when you first become conscious in the morning, get decent. She awakes and goes through the following routine: looks over the day's calendar; warms up and exercises; showers; puts on make-up; fixes hair; and puts on clothes. She says she is then ready to meet God and the day's agenda.

I realize not everyone can do this and you have to work out a plan that works best for you. It may help to set out the clothes you plan to wear the night before. Make sure they are pressed and ready to slip on. It also may mean getting up a little earlier to beat your husband or children to the shower.

Getting ready early makes us ready to face the day ahead. I can accomplish more when I look my best because I feel better about myself. Also it may help our husbands. As they think of us during the day their last memory of us is pleasant. They left a wife who did her best to look nice for him rather than a woman with a robe on, curlers in her hair, and a sleepy look in her eye. It helps their self-esteem as well as ours to know we take enough pride in ourselves to look our best throughout the day.

6. **Do what you can to improve your appearance**, *and don't worry about the things that cannot be changed.* As you examine your list of areas that need work, put a star by the areas you can change. Then get busy. Set goals for yourself. (For example, I will lose twenty pounds by October; or I will exercise fifteen minutes each day.) Try to work on your appearance a little while each day and build your confidence. Don't forget your "assets!"

Now look at your list and see if you listed any physical features that cannot be changed. (For instance, your height or the shape of your face). Mark those things off your list so you will not worry about them. After all, that is what Jesus said to do in Matthew 6. Let your inner beauty radiate and people soon won't notice if you are too tall or have a big nose.

My husband, Gary, is only five feet five inches tall. He is always hearing short people jokes, but he laughs and goes on. He said he learned a long time ago that he cannot help being short or change it, so he does not let it bother him. (Of course, in my eyes, Gary is ten feet tall!) His life far makes up for his height. Do the best you can with what you have.

Conclusion

Our appearance has a tremendous influence on how we feel about ourselves and how others feel about us. Our beauty must first come from within, realizing God looks at our hearts. We should do what we can to look our best outwardly. When we feel like we have done the best we can with our appearance, we should not worry. We have confidence that as Christian women we are beautiful in God's eyes.

For Thought & Discussion

▦ 1. Break into small discussion groups of four to six people. Take each member of the group and have the other members point out:

    a) Qualities of inner beauty which they possess

    b) Some physical assets they possess ("You have beautiful blue eyes, fingernails," etc.)

▦ 2. Have each member of the discussion group share one aspect of her appearance she would like to work on. Encourage one another.

▦ 3. Discuss as a class how important physical beauty should be to the Christian. Talk about how the world reflects its attitude toward beauty.

▦ 4. Make a list of qualities that make the Christian woman beautiful from within. Give examples of beautiful Christian women and what makes them beautiful.

▦ 5. How can we help our children when someone makes fun of their appearance? How do we teach them not to judge others by their appearance?

▦ 6. List examples of beautiful women of the Bible.

▦ 7. What are some actions and attitudes that detract from a woman's beauty?

▦ 8. Make a poster that shows the contrast of a woman who is beautiful inwardly and a woman who may be beautiful outwardly but not in heart.

▦ 9. Make a list of consultants, books, etc., that might advise us on how to improve our appearance.

PART II: SELF-ESTEEM BUILDERS

6

A Right Relationship With God

PART 1

The last four chapters have looked at what we considered self-esteem destroyers. These were the influences that Christian women felt caused them to have a poor self-esteem. We discussed how they affect us and what we can do to overcome their negative impact on our lives. The remainder of the book will discuss self-esteem builders. Using the results of our survey, we will study the things that help Christian women have a positive, high self-esteem.

I believe God wants us to have a good self-esteem. We are His ambassadors. If the world sees that we have no self-confidence and a low opinion of ourselves, then we probably are not very good representatives for God. Paul wrote, "Be imitators of me as I am of Christ" (I Corinthians 11:1). Could we say that? Does our life reflect enough joy and confidence in Christ that we would want someone to imitate it? It should!

Notice I asked if our lives reflect joy and confidence *in Christ*. That is the key to the Christian's self-esteem! A good self-esteem is one that is based on a right relationship with God. That was the answer listed most often in our survey. When asked what had the greatest influence on helping you have a good self-esteem, forty-one percent listed a good relationship with God as their first choice. That explains the big difference between the self-esteem of a Christian and someone who is not a Christian. Their self-esteems are based on two completely different things.

The non-Christians must base their self-esteem on "self." Their feelings about themselves may be influenced by their appearance, intelligence, wealth or personality. The Christian may be influenced by those things, but the basis for their self-esteem comes not from "self" but from God. The Christian can have a high self-esteem because of who God is and what He has done for us. As we grow in our relationship with God, we feel better about ourselves and grow in our confidence. It is not because of who we are or what we have done but because of what God can do with our lives when we commit them to Him.

As we continue to grow in our relationship with God, He equips us to combat the influences that attack our self-esteem. The world does not have that defense. Through God we can overcome guilt, anxiety, fear, criticism, worldliness and the other self-esteem destroyers. Perhaps self-esteem is not the best choice of words. Maybe it should be "God's esteem." He should receive the glory as He helps us grow. Our confidence is not really self-confidence but confidence in God because of what He has done for us.

In order to have the confidence that comes from God, we must first recognize who God is and who we are without Him. When we understand that, we must desire to grow in our relationship with Him and allow God to mold our lives. The remainder of this chapter will discuss who God is and who we are. The following chapter will deal with building a good relationship with God.

Who Is God?
Have you ever had to describe God to someone? What would you say if you were asked to introduce God to someone who has never heard of Him? Would it be difficult? Do we really know who God is, or is He a figurehead or a fairytale-like character who has been handed down since childhood?

How would you draw a picture of God? When I was teaching first grade, one of my students brought me a picture she had drawn. It was a typical first-grade picture with a house, trees, and flowers, but this picture also had three red hearts in the sky. I called the student back to my desk and asked her why she had put the three hearts in the sky. She replied, "Mrs. McKnight, that is God. You told us God is love." That is one picture I have not thrown away.

Let us examine some of the words the Bible uses to describe God. There are many. *Nave's Topical Bible* uses eighty-eight pages to state the verses that describe who God is and what He is like. We will only look at six descriptions.

1. **God is the Creator.** (Genesis 1 and 2, Ecclesiastes 3:11) The verse in Ecclesiastes says that man cannot fathom what God has done from the beginning. We certainly see the evidence of that today as scientists try to disprove God's creation with evolution. Perhaps God did not mean for us to understand how He created things. We can only accept what the Bible tells us, "God said, Let there be...."

God created man. Not only did He create us, but He made us in His image (Genesis 1:26). Have you ever thought what it means to be made in the image of God? Nothing else was created in His image. From the beginning, God made man special. (What does that do for your self-esteem?)

Because God made us, He knows what is best for us and has given us instructions for happiness in His Word. Often, when a watch is broken, we must send it back to the factory, its maker, for repairs. When our lives are broken, we too must return to our Maker. God can repair our lives.

2. **God is our Father.** (I John 3:1, Isaiah 64:8) Think of some of the characteristics of earthly fathers that make them so dear to us. Our fathers provided for us, taught us, disciplined us, loved us, advised us, and gave us their name.

Compare this with God. He too provides for us, teaches us, disciplines us, loves us, advises us, and allows us to be called His children. We even wear His son's name, Christian. When we think of the love earthly fathers have for their children, we begin to understand just a portion of God's love for us. John Gipson described it in the following article:

My father supplied me with thoughtful care. One of the joys of childhood was the absence of care concerning where I was going to live, what I was going to eat, and what I was going to wear. Though I grew up in the Great Depression, I never had a care. I knew that my father could be depended upon to take care of my every need. My childhood days were happy and carefree. I didn't know what it meant to worry. I'm glad that I have a Heavenly Father who promises "all of these things shall be yours..." (Matthew 6:33). Oh, that I might once again have the childlike faith in God which I placed in my father. With the kind of daddy I had, this lesson should be easy for me.

I'm thankful for the *wise guidance* of my father. He showed me how to saw a straight line, nail up sheetrock, hang a door, hunt quail, drive a car, plant a garden, do my arithmetic, pray before meals, and a thousand and one other things I wasn't even aware of. He not only told me what to do, he actually showed me. How thankful I am that I have a Heavenly Father who is willing to guide me with His counsel and set the pattern in love, righteousness, mercy, pity, etc. He not only tells the way — He shows me.

I'm grateful for the *loving discipline* of my father. From time to time he dealt with my fighting, smoking, stealing, stubbornness, etc., with counsel, a belt, sunflower stalks or the removal of his approval. His discipline was not pleasant, but ever merciful. So with God. "For the Lord disciplines him who he loves, and chastises every son whom he receives" (Hebrews 12:6). I'm thankful that God treats me as a son. It's for my good.

I'm thankful for the *maturing trust* my father placed in me. He trusted me with his money, his shotgun, his car, his jobs, his name. I am ashamed that I didn't always live up to that trust, but I will always be thankful for his confidence. I'm glad God treats me in the same way. It's His world, His name and His work, but He's entrusted them all to me.

I'm thankful for a dedicated father who has taught me so many wonderful things about God. I'm a child of God. I have received the spirit of sonship. And it is with joy I cry, "Abba Father!"   University Church of Christ Bulletin
Tuscaloosa, Alabama

3. God is our Savior. (Isaiah 12:2) Without God as our savior we have no hope of eternal life. We do not deserve a savior, and it is hard to comprehend how God could love us enough to want to save us. It is a demonstration of His grace through Jesus. He became our savior even when we did not deserve it.

Before we can understand what it means to have a savior, we must recognize our need for a savior. We must understand that we are lost and must allow God, through our obedience, to save us.

4. God is our Guide. (Psalm 48:14) What a comfort it is to know we have someone to lead us and guide us on our journey through life! God is often compared to a shepherd. We see in John 10:2-4 how a shepherd leads his sheep. He does not drive them, but goes ahead of them and they follow the shepherd.

God does not drive people and make them go against their will. He has offered His guidance, but we must be willing to follow. Too many times we want God to be our savior, but we want to be the guide. Real happiness comes when we stop trying to lead and let God guide us (Luke 10:23-24).

5. God is our King. (I Timothy 6:15-16) There is something about royalty that draws immediate attention and grandeur. Can you recall the royal wedding of Prince Charles and Lady Diana in July 1981 and the publicity given to the birth of their son? All the gala associated with royalty cannot compare to having an immortal king like God.

Earthly kingdoms rise and fall. (Just read I and II Kings!) God's kingdom is eternal. As our king, He has complete authority. Daniel 6:26 and Matthew 19:26 describe His sovereign power. We know God's kingdom will never fail.

Our understanding of God as a king must begin by allowing Him to rule our individual lives. Is He the lord (master) of your life? We must honor His authority and the authority of His Word by submitting and obeying it.

6. God is our Judge. (Hebrews 10:30; Ecclesiastes 12:14) Many people become fearful when they think of God's judgment. It is interesting to hear how differently people describe what they think God will say to them at the Judgment Day.

The Christians have no reason to fear God as their judge. What better judge could we have than someone who is also our creator, father, and savior! God's love will extend into His justice and mercy. The Christian can rejoice and look forward to having God as his judge.

What Is God Like?

Building a good relationship with someone requires knowing that individual well. Not only could you describe their physical characteristics, but you could describe their inward qualities as well. The same is true with God. We must know the characteristics that make Him God.

Below are listed some of the characteristics of God that we read in the Scriptures. As you study these characteristics, think about how you have seen these characteristics demonstrated in the lives of Bible characters and in your life. Which of these characteristics mean a lot to you personally when you think of God?

CHARACTERISTICS OF GOD:

1. **Accessible** (Hebrews 4:16; Ephesians 3:12). We can approach God and communicate with Him at any time.

2. **Holy** (Revelation 15:4). God is characterized by perfection that commands absolute adoration and reverence.

3. **Goodness** (Psalm 119:68). God demonstrates excellence and virtue.

4. **Righteous / Just** (Psalm 145:17). God is fair and reasonable in accordance with what is correct.

5. **Compassionate** (Psalm 145:8). God is sympathetic. He is aware of people's distress and desires to eliminate it.

6. **Merciful** (Psalm 103:8). God is willing to forbear punishment for the Christian even when justice demands it.

7. **Longsuffering** (II Peter 3:9,15). God's patience and endurance cannot compare with any we have known on earth.

8. **Faithful** (I Corinthians 1:9). God is loyal and constant. He will never change.

9. **Impartial** (I Peter 1:17; Colossians 3:25). God shows no favoritism. His love is extended to all.

10. **Love** (I John 4:8-10). God is love. He demonstrated the highest form of love in sacrificing His Son for us. His love is "agape" in which he seeks the best for all.

I urge you to study these and other characteristics of God more carefully. Try to come to a greater understanding of how God demonstrates these qualities and what they really mean. Make a greater effort to get to know God better and allow Him to become a closer, better friend. It is only when we know God that we really can know ourselves.

Who Are We?

The Christian's self-esteem comes from a realization of what we were without God compared with what we are with God. It is quite a contrast.

1. **We were sinners.** We read in Romans 3:23 that all have sinned and fallen short of the glory of God. I John 1:8 warns those who claim to be without sin and tells them they are only deceiving themselves.

When we were living in a sinful condition, we must recognize that we were separated from the God we just described. "The sinful mind is hostile to God. It does not submit to God's law, nor can it do so. Those controlled by the sinful nature cannot please God" (Romans 8:7-8). It is not pleasant to think about being separated from God's love, mercy, and forgiveness.

2. **We were lost.** Without God, we were separated from His spiritual blessings on earth. We also were separated from the hope of eternal life. We often sing "Amazing Grace... I once was lost but now I'm found...."

Jesus taught that people would be lost eternally and describes the separation in Matthew 25:41-46. He even warns that some who are religious will be lost (Matthew 7:21-23). How sad it is to bear the burden and guilt of sin and be separated from God.

People who are lost have no reason to have a high self-esteem. They may seek the things that the world believes are important, but Luke 16:15 tells us, "What is highly valued among men is detestable in God's sight." No wonder so many search for happiness and a sense of worth but never find it without God.

It is different for the Christian. We were sinners and lost at one point, but we believed God's Word (Hebrews 11:6), repented of our sins (Luke 13:3), confessed Jesus is Lord (Romans 10:9-10), and were baptized for the remission of our sins (Acts 2:38). We took on a new name, new attitudes, new goals, and a new perspective of life and God. No longer are we considered sinners and lost.

3. Now **we are children of God** (I John 3:1). When we became Christians we took on a new family. As a child of God we are members of His family, the church (I Corinthians 12:12-27). We are also God's heirs (Romans 8:16-17). Did you ever think you would be an heir of a king. You are, if you are a Christian! How does that make you feel?

4. **We are light.** The Bible often compares Christians with light and the world with darkness. Paul reminded the Ephesians, "You were once darkness, but now you are light in the Lord. Live as children of light" (Ephesians 5:8). Jesus taught that we are the light of the world (Matthew 5:14-16) and He gave us a job to do. We are to be proud of our light and let it shine in the world so they too may come to know God.

5. **We are saved** (I John 5:13). We don't have to wonder if we will inherit eternal life. We can know it! Too many Christians lack confidence in their salvation. If you cannot confidently say, "I know I am going to heaven," you need to sit down and get to know God better and examine His Word. Doubts will only hinder your relationship with God and your feelings about yourself. Confidence in our salvation comes from knowing God's Word and obeying it daily.

Conclusion

Hopefully, we have seen that the basis for the Christian's self-esteem is God. We must also realize that we were lost, but now we are God's children. The blessings that spring from being children of God give us a greater feeling of self-worth. We are not confident in ourselves, but in God.

> When you surrender to Christ, all self-hate, all self-loathing, all self-rejection drops away. How can you hate what He loves? How can you reject what He accepts? How can you look down on what He died for? You are no longer a person, you are 'a person for whom Christ died.' If He died for me, there must be something in me worth dying for. So surrender to Christ saves you, on the one hand, from self-assertion, always wanting to occupy the center of attention, and on the other hand, from shyness which is always shrinking and thinking, 'what do they think of me?' ...You are not a worm, not a wonder. You are the ordinary becoming the extraordinary, all due to Him. So you can be yourself because you are His self. You are free to be.
>
> E. Stanley Jones, quoted by Bruce Narramore in *You're Someone Special*

For Thought & Discussion

▨ 1. Divide the class into small groups. Have each group discuss one of the characteristics that describes God. Find biblical examples where this characteristic is demonstrated. Discuss how you have seen it work in people's lives today. How does this characteristic affect your self-esteem?

▨ 2. Using Bible reference materials, find other words that describe who God is and what He is like. Share some of the Psalms that describe God.

▨ 3. Have individuals share the difference in their self-esteem before and after they became a Christian.

▨ 4. How do Christians show the world their basis for a good self-esteem without being boastful or self-righteous? Discuss the Christian's role as a light.

▨ 5. Make a chart contrasting our lives before and after we become Christians. Include biblical comparisons, difference in attitudes, goals, lifestyles, etc.

"BEFORE CHRIST"   "AFTER CHRIST"

▨ 6. Compare the difference in how children view God and how adults view Him. Have class members who teach Bible classes or have small children ask their children to describe God.

▨ 7. Reread I Corinthians 11:1. List specific ways we can imitate Christ. How does our self-esteem influence the way we imitate Christ?

7

A Right Relationship With God

PART 2

In chapter 6 we discussed how a right relationship with God is the most basic ingredient to the Christian woman's self-esteem. We examined who God is and compared our lives with God and without God. This chapter will continue to examine our relationship with God in a more practical way. We will see how we can build a better relationship with God and how this can build our self-esteem. Once again, let me remind you that a good self-esteem isn't based on who we are, but on what God has made us.

Many Christian women realize this. Forty-one percent of those surveyed said a good relationship with God was the most important self-esteem builder in their lives. It is interesting to note that ninety percent of the women who rated their self-esteem as very high (eight or above) engage in personal prayer and Bible study at least several times a week. Over half said they have quiet times daily. There seems to be a direct correlation between our relationship with God, our prayer and Bible study habits, and our self-esteem. How can we improve our relationship with God?

Get Rid Of Barriers

Before we build a good relationship with God, we must get in a right relationship with Him. This requires self-examination.

"Examine yourselves to see whether you are in the faith; test yourselves. Do you realize that Christ is in you — unless, of course, you fail the test?" (II Corinthians 13:5)

Ask yourself, "Have I believed completely in God's Word and confessed Jesus as His son? Did I really repent of my sins and make a change in my life? Have I put on Christ in baptism? Have I accepted God's forgiveness and forgiven myself? Am I living my life in obedience to God's will? Are there any barriers that stand in the way of my relationship with God?

We must be very honest with ourselves and with God when we answer these questions. If we realize there are some barriers to the relationship, we need to admit them and ask God to help us get rid of them. What are some barriers?

1.   **Sin.** We know that sin separates us from God, and God hates sin. Hebrews 12:1-2 compares the Christian life to running a race. Just as a competitive runner sheds his warm-up suit or other heavy clothing to run a race, the Christian must shed any sin. The Hebrews writer says sin entangles us and takes our eyes off Jesus.

Satan is so creative, patient, and powerful. He can so easily catch us off our guard and trap us in sin before we realize it. We must continually examine our lives for those "quiet sins" such as jealousy, bad attitudes, selfishness, gossip, greed, pride and neglect.

If there is a sin hindering your relationship with God, deal with it. Confess it to God in prayer and ask His forgiveness and strength to overcome it. Then each day try to build a better relationship with God.

2. **Dependence on self.** Another barrier to a good relationship with God is depending on yourself rather than God. Find someone who worries a great deal and you probably have found someone who is still depending on themselves.

Self-dependence is basically a lack of faith. In essence we are saying, "God, I'm not sure You can handle this or that You would want to hear about it. I'll take care of it myself." We will never have a good relationshp with God as long as we are still trying to control our lives. He wants to be our lord and master (Acts 2:26), and we must submit in faith.

3. **Lack of time.** Isn't it odd that God is the giver of time, yet we often say we don't have time for Him? Any relationship requires time if the relationship is to grow and be worthwhile. Marriages in which partners don't take time for one another often end in divorce. Parents must take time for their children or the relationship suffers. The same is true with God. If we don't take time with God each day, the relationship will suffer.

We are busy people. We have homes to keep, husbands to love, children to care for, appointments to meet, jobs to go to, meals to cook, and on and on it goes. We have allowed our lives to become so hectic and busy that we often crowd out the Giver of time itself. How sad!

We sing "Take Time To Be Holy," and that is exactly what we must do. We find time to do exactly what we want to do. If building a better relationship with God is important to us, we will find time for Him. It may mean waking up earlier, staying up later, using our hours more efficiently, or eliminating some activities. It is a matter of priorities. How much do I need God? How important is it to me to study, pray, and worship?

If a lack of time is a barrier for you (and it probably is for most of us), I hope some of the suggestions made throughout the rest of this chapter can help.

Improve Your Communication With God

One key to any worthwhile relationship is to establish good communication. Marriage counselors tell us that marriages begin to crumble when a husband and wife fail to communicate with one another. We sometimes become so busy tending to our families' physical needs that we don't take time to listen and talk about their emotional or spiritual needs. Misunderstandings are frequent in relationships where there is poor communication. Think of how many friendships have been dissolved when one friend moves away and no one writes, calls or visits. In time the friends lose touch or remember each other only with a Christmas card.

Our relationship with God also requires good communication. We are too often like the friends who lose touch. We only occasionally offer a prayer or read the Bible. God isn't the friend who moves. We are. He is always there and always communicating.

God has communicated with us from the beginning of time. (Doesn't that make you feel special?) We see Him talking with Adam and Eve in the Garden, sending angels to Abraham, using plagues to warn Egypt, and sending prophets to Judah and Israel. In the New Testament we see His communication in sending Christ and then giving the Holy Spirit to intercede for us (Romans 8:26-27). Today, God is still communicating with us through His Word, the Bible. God talks to us and desires that we listen.

Good communication requires good listening skills. How much do we listen to God by spending time studying and reading the Bible outside of church? Think about the past week or two and see if you can measure the time you spent reading God's Word. Have we reached a point where we are hungering and thirsting after righteousness (Matthew 5:6)? Do we feel that we really need God's words each day of our lives? Do we turn to the Bible in times of joy, thanksgiving, distress and tragedy? Is the Bible meaningful to us, and do we make it applicable? Can we find passages easily or quote verses from memory? Do we feel a greater sense of peace, strength and confidence after reading the Bible? Do we really consider that God is talking to us personally?

The following is written in the front of my Bible. It serves as a reminder that God has spoken to all of the needs in our life if we will only stop and listen.

READ

When in sorrow . . . . John 14

When men fail you . . . . Psalm 27

When you have sinned . . . . Psalm 51

When you worry . . . . Matthew 6:19-34

Before church services . . . . Psalm 84

When you are in danger . . . . Psalm 91

When you have the blues . . . . Psalm 34

When God seems far away . . . . Psalm 139

We must also remember that good communication involves two. God has spoken to us, and He is also willing to listen to us. He wants us to talk to Him in prayer. I can write the President a letter or phone him, but his aides will reply. It is not that way with God. We can talk with Him directly at any time and any place! Isn't that wonderful! (That should give your self-esteem a boost!)

God gave us such a good example of what our prayer life should be in Jesus. Jesus' apostles asked Him to teach them how to pray (Luke 11:1). They saw a relationship between Jesus' prayer life and His ministry. Jesus went to a solitary place at daybreak to pray (Luke 4:42). He withdrew from crowds to go to a lonely place to pray (Luke 5:16). On one occasion He spent all night in prayer (Luke 6:12).

How about us? Are we willing to get up earlier to pray? Do we find quiet places where we can leave distractions behind us and pray? Do we feel the need to pray? Can we pray in times of rejoi-cing, or do we only pray when trouble arises? Do we talk to God openly and really cast our cares on Him? How persistent are our prayers (Luke 18:1-8)? Do we pray with confidence and faith, knowing God will answer (I John 5:14-15; Ephesians 3:20, John 15:7)? Have you seen your prayers answered? Are we willing to let go of our worries and cares and turn them completely over to God? Do we take time to pray? Does our prayer life affect our feelings about ourselves?

I Didn't have time

I got up early one morning
And rushed right into the day;
I had so much to accomplish
That I didn't have time to pray.

Problems came tumbling about me,
And heavier came each task.
Why doesn't God help? I wondered,
He answered, "You didn't ask."

I wanted to see joy and beauty,
But the day toiled on, grey and bleak.
I wondered why God didn't show me;
He said, "But you didn't seek."

I tried to come into God's presence,
I used all my keys in the lock.
God gently and lovingly chided,
"My child, you didn't knock."

I woke up early this morning
And prayed before entering the day;
I had so much to accomplish
That I had to take time to pray.

—AUTHOR UNKNOWN

When a native in Uganda accepted Christ, he was told to select a quiet spot in the bush for his daily devotions. As he went there daily, a path was worn in the grass. But the grass grew rapidly. If he missed a day, the grass grew a little higher. If he continued to miss his quiet time the path completely disappeared. The spiritual condition of the natives was gauged by their prayer paths. Do we have distinct prayer paths into God's presence or has the grass grown over them because we have neglected to communicate with God?

Our relationship with God largely depends on our willingness to take time to communicate with Him. Our quiet times with God are not a duty. They should be considered a privilege.

Practical Suggestions
For Improving Communication

Below are some practical suggestions that may help us improve our communication with God. Perhaps one or more of them can help you.

1. **Decide what you want to study.** There are so many ways to study the Bible and so many areas to study. Each person must decide what is best for his needs and what will help him the most in his spiritual growth.

You may wish to spend your study time finding scriptures on a specific topic that is important to you or meets a particular need in your life. Or you may choose to study one book of the Bible in depth. I have a friend who spent one month studying the book of Ephesians. Even though Ephesians only has six chapters she devoted the whole month to its study by reading the book in its entirety, studying it verse by verse, memorizing important passages, reading commentaries, and comparing versions. There can be much more involved in study than merely reading.

You may desire to spend your study time preparing for a class you teach or studying for a class you attend. Can you imagine the difference in our Bible classes if each student came with his lesson studied in advance? We often expect the teacher to do all the studying and then just fill us up with knowledge. Every Christian should desire to study and contribute to his class.

You can use your study time to review notes from sermons. We read in Acts 17:11 that the Bereans studied to see if what they were being taught was right. We should never take the preacher's word as truth without examining in in God's Word.

Some choose to use devotional books or aides in their quiet times. I know one girl who reads one chapter of Proverbs each day. She said there is a chapter for each day of the month and it helps her live better if she reads it continually.

Your needs will change. You must study what is best for you. The important thing is **study!** Allow God to talk to you.

2. **Try to set a specific time for study and prayer.** Once again, everyone is different and must suit their time for what is best for them. Many have a quiet time early in the morning to set the tone for the day. This requires disciplining yourself enough to wake up earlier and not linger in bed. Others prefer late at night just before bedtime. (Be careful and don't fall asleep while you are praying.) Having a specific time is like making an appointment with God. We are less likely to let the day slip by without study and prayer if we make that appointment time a habit. It becomes a very special time of day.

3. **Learn to use small amounts of time wisely.** After our son, Jonathan, was born I became very frustrated because my set study time was gone. I often wondered where those blocks of quiet time went. Children demand so much of our time. We must be willing to adjust and change, but we must never lose the desire to spend time with God.

During the day we engage in many activities which are actually wasted "mind space." We are physically doing something (vacuuming, washing dishes, drying our hair, etc.) but our minds are not busy. We can use these times to communicate with God. Since Jonathan's birth I have learned to pray in the shower or while I'm drying my hair. We can pray while we're driving or rocking a baby. I believe God understands if our eyes aren't closed or our heads bowed. We can tape Bible verses above the kitchen sink or on mirrors and think about them or memorize them as we wash dishes or get ready. I know of a lady who asked her husband to buy her the tapes of the Bible for Christmas. She listens to the tapes while she irons, cooks, and paints.

We have periods of time where we are required to wait, such as in a doctor's office. This is a great time to review class notes, sermon outlines or read a religious book. It takes our minds off waiting. Then there are those five and ten minute time slots during the day which are free. On Wednesday evenings I usually have ten to fifteen minutes between the time I get the kitchen clean and time to leave for church. This is a great time to review my lesson for Bible class and get my mind ready for worship. We waste too many of these short time slots in front of the television set.

4. **Organize your prayer requests into a prayer list.** This suggestion helped me tremendously. It helped me to pray more specifically and remember others' needs. It also helped me to see how many prayers God has answered. If you keep your prayer lists over a period of time and mark off prayers as they are answered, it will build your faith and confidence in prayer tremendously.

You may wish to divide your prayer list into categories. You could list the sick together. Have categories for such things as non-Christians you are praying for, friends' needs, church matters, and personal requests. After you make the list, *pray, pray, pray* and *pray specifically* for the people on your list. Keep your list updated.

The ladies of our congregation worked together on a prayer list at our ladies' retreat. We helped each other become aware of members' needs and desires that needed praying for. We included those who were sick and shut-in, those who desired to have a baby, those who wanted a Christian husband, marriages that were in trouble, names of spouses and friends who weren't Christians, church activities (gospel meetings, Bible school programs, etc.), our missionaries, decisions, jobs and on and on. We prayed as a group and then encouraged one another to pray for these things individually on a regular basis. At our next retreat we stopped and talked about how many of our prayers had been answered and we made prayer requests again.

Recently I looked at my personal prayer list and wondered why so many requests were unanswered. Then I examined my prayer life and realized it was I who had failed. I had become negligent in prayer. There is tremendous power in prayer, but only if we ask. *God is listening.*

Conclusion

We have discussed how to build a better relationship with God by getting rid of barriers that hinder the relationship and improving our communication with God. How does this affect your self-esteem?

We grow closer to God by understanding who He is and what He has done for us and by spending more time communicating with Him through studying the Bible and prayer. When this happens, we begin to rely more on God and less on ourselves. We see God as our source of wisdom and strength and allow Him to guide us. As we see our prayers answered, we become more and more confident in God. We place our life in His hands and know He will meet every need. This confidence in God gives us a feeling of security and inner peace. We can feel good about ourselves because we are in a right relationship with God.

For Thought & Discussion

▓ 1. Give additional Biblical examples of how God has communicated with people. Find and read some examples of prayers people prayed in the Bible.

▓ 2. Have your class make a prayer list. Update your list each week and encourage one another to pray more. Make special note of the prayers that are answered each week.

▓ 3. How do we demonstrate dependence on self rather than God? How can we help one another overcome this barrier?

▓ 4. Have various class members share how they conduct their quiet time. What do they study? When do they study?

▓ 5. Make out a schedule of your day for a week. Study it. How can you better organize your time to allow more time to communicate with God?

▓ 6. Discuss how your relationship with God contributes to your self-esteem. How can a better relationship with God improve your self-esteem?

▓ 7. Make a commitment to do at least one thing that will improve your relationship with God. Write your commitment down and pray about it.

8

Good Family Relationships

PART 1

The last two chapters discussed how a good relationship with God is the foundation for the Christian woman's good self-esteem. There are also other elements that help us build a good self-esteem. One element that has a great influence is our families. Our survey showed that thirty percent of the women felt their early family background had the greatest influence on their good self-esteem. Nine percent credited their good self-esteem to their present family situation. When asked which people had helped them build a good self-esteem, forty-seven percent said their parents had helped the most and twenty-six percent said their husbands. Certainly, it is clear that our families have a tremendous influence on the way we feel about ourselves.

Families may not always help us have a positive self-concept. Twelve percent of the women surveyed said it was their parents who caused them to have a poor self-esteem and five percent blamed their husbands. Early family background ranked fourth among the influences toward a poor self-esteem.

We will spend the next two chapters examining the importance of the family in building not only our self-esteem but also the self-esteem of our parents, husbands, and children. In this chapter we will discuss the effects of our early family background. We will also discuss how we as women set the emotional tone for our present families' self-esteem. Chapter nine will deal more specifically with how we can build good self-esteem in our children.

Your Early Family Background

In 1959 Ross Laboratories published a pamphlet for parents entitled "Developing Self-Esteem." The following is a quotation from that pamphlet:

> We humans possess a capacity that is unique among living creatures. Each of us has an awareness of himself as an individual. Each has developed this awareness through a gradually increasing ability to obtain satisfaction from the surroundings by his own efforts and because those close to him in the growing-up years looked on him as a special, distinct person.
>
> The way in which we were regarded in those early years determines to a great extent the esteem we now have of ourselves as adults. The feeling that we have dignity and worthwhileness as persons provides a healthy soil for the growth of self-confidence. But regarding ourselves as unworthy or bumbling persons—a feeling that develops from belittling attitudes toward us in our early years—can plague us unhappily throughout life. Most of us look at ourselves with a mixture of respect and scorn, because there was a mixture of accepting and deprecating attitudes shown toward us in our childhood.

We cannot deny the fact that what we experienced as children affects us all of our lives. Child development specialists tell us a child's basic personality is usually formed by the time he begins school. But it is after a child enters school that his self-esteem usually comes under attack. Children can be cruel to one another and parents must continually rebuild their children's self-esteem.

Think back to your own childhood. What are some specific things your parents did to build your self-esteem? How did they teach you to react when unkind remarks were said? Did your parents point you continually to God and His love?

If you were blessed with Christian parents who helped you form a high self-esteem while you were young, thank them. Thank God for them! In return, build their self-esteem by telling them what good parents they were and how much you love them. As they grow older, do all you can to make them feel worthwhile and valuable. Show your parents you appreciate them by phone calls, cards, and letters. Learn to express your love for them. Help their "olden years" be "golden years." (Read I Timothy 5:3-4.) Our love and respect for our parents does not end when we leave home. It is usually after we leave that we really learn to appreciate all they have done for us.

My parents have done so much for me. My goal as a parent is to be the kind of parent they were for me. I hope to train my children spiritually by following their example. I always knew God was the most important thing in their lives and they lived Matthew 6:33 daily. They trained my sister and me to love to go to church and read God's Word. Prayer was a vital part of each day, and we learned to rejoice together as we saw prayers answered. Even after leaving home, I have been encouraged by them in so many ways. This book is partly a result of their support and belief that I could do it. I could go on and on.... They built my self-esteem by providing a spiritual atmosphere at home.

I often wish I could buy my parents expensive gifts to express my love for them, but the money isn't there. I know a weekly letter, a picture of the grandchildren, and verbal expressions of love mean more than any gift. Perhaps the greatest gift we can give our parents is the assurance they have trained their children to live godly lives. Our lives should reflect that they have been successful parents. That makes them feel worthy.

Overcoming A Poor Background
We must be realistic and understand that not everyone had the privilege of being raised in a family situation that promotes good self-esteem. Remember, twelve percent said their parents had caused them to have a poor self-esteem. What can you do if you find yourself in that situation? Are you "doomed" to have low self-esteem?

Many drown themselves in self-pity. They feel that they have good reason to have low self-esteem. As a result they sit and mope and expect everyone to feel sorry for them and say, "She's had a hard life." We cannot change our early background. All the self-pity and tears will not make it different. We can allow a poor family background to handicap us all our lives or we can learn from it and compensate.

Victor and Mildred Goertzel conducted a famous study entitled "Cradles of Eminence" in which they investigated the home backgrounds of four hundred highly successful individuals who had made it to the top. Three-fourths of the backgrounds they investigated revealed childhoods troubled by poverty, broken homes, rejection, overpossessiveness, financial ups and downs, physical handicaps or parental dissatisfaction. One-fourth of those investigated had handicaps such as blindness, deafness, being crippled, homely, overweight, undersized or having a speech defect. How did they get to be successful? They learned to compensate.

There is a popular poster out today that says, "When life hands you a lemon, make lemonade." That is compensation. It is finding good in bad situations. Romans 8:28 says, "All things work together for good to them that love God and are called according to His promises." It does not say "All things are good," but it does promise things will work together for good. It may take years to see the good come. God may desire that you use your poor family background to empathize and help others. We often question why things happen, but God may be using our painful experiences to prepare us to bear the burdens of others. Dr. James Dobson says the Christian principle of bearing one another's burdens offers the best solution to inferiority and inadequacy. He states,

> *I have repeatedly observed that a person's own needs and problems seem less threatening when he is busy helping someone else handle theirs! It is difficult to wallow in your own troubles when you are actively shouldering another person's load and seeking solutions to his problems. For each discouraged reader who feels unloved and short-changed by life, I would recommend that you consciously make a practice of giving yourself to others.*

There are so many who need you and who can profit from your experiences. You are in an excellent position to empathize with others. Look for things to do for others (Colossians 4:5). There are sick people, shut-ins and newcomers to visit. There are those who need phone calls and notes of encouragement. Many are lonely and just desire someone to talk to. As you give to others, your sense of uselessness will begin to fade. You will help yourself and others as well.

Certainly our early family background plays an important role in our self-esteem. If your family background gave you a high self-esteem, build on it. If your family hindered your self-esteem, don't drown yourself in self-pity. Remember that God is the basic foundation of our self-esteem. You can still have a good self-esteem because of Him.

Self-Esteem: A Family Affair

Time and time again I have heard ministers say, "Although the man is to be the leader in the home, it is the woman who usually sets the emotional tone for the family." As wives and mothers we have a tremendous influence on the self-esteem of our husbands and children. Our attitudes, temperament and the way we feel about ourselves are often reflected in the lives of our families.

I have found that on days when I feel pressured or irritable, our small son, Jonathan, is much more likely to be fussy and demand attention. If we greet our husbands when they come home from work with all our problems, their morale is likely to be affected. An older Christian lady recently shared that she knew her husband's mood by the way he came in. If he came directly to her she knew he had had a good day, but if he went to their bedroom and removed his coat and tie first she knew he had had a rough day. She realized her response to him was very important and she reacted according to his entrance.

Christian women are continually reminded of the virtuous woman described in Proverbs 31. We know nothing of her early family background, but I can't help believing that she was a woman with high self-esteem. Verse twenty-eight tells us her children called her blessed and her husband praised her. Verse thirty-one says her works are even to be praised in the city gate. What had made this woman so deserving of praise and honor? She wasn't famous and did nothing spectacular.

First of all, she is worthy of praise because she feared the Lord (verse 30). Does that sound familiar? Our self-esteem is based on a right relationship with God. It wasn't her charm or beauty that made her feel worthwhile, but her fear of the Lord.

Proverbs 31:10 says the virtuous woman is worth far more than rubies. Consider her worth to her husband. He has full confidence in her (verse 11) and she brings him good all the days of her life (verse 12). As a result, he is respected at the city gate (verse 23).

Consider her worth to her children. She arises early to prepare food for her family (verse 15), and she continues to work vigorously all day (verses 17 and 18). She is well-prepared to clothe her family (verse 21), and she watches over the affairs of her household (verse 27).

Consider her worth to others. She opens her arms to the poor and extends her hand to the needy (verse 20). She demonstrates wisdom in dealing with merchants (verses 16, 18, and 24). She teaches and speaks with wisdom (verse 26).

It is hard to imagine this virtuous woman having a poor self-esteem and feeling unworthy. She could have a sense of worthiness because she was unselfish. Her fear of the Lord was demonstrated through her relationship with others. She set a beautiful example for us to follow in establishing the proper emotional tone for our families.

What about you? Does your husband have confidence in you? Can you say you bring him good and help him to be respected at work, the church, and the community? Are you a hard, diligent worker for your family? Does your family see you helping those in need? Do you take time to teach your children and laugh with your family? Do you speak with wisdom? What kind of emotional tone do you set for your family? Is it one that encourages good self-esteem?

If we are busy serving others and building their self-esteem, our self-esteem will improve. It is a reciprocal response. Remember, the result of the virtuous woman's work and efforts for her family and others was praise. They built up her self-esteem with proper respect and honor.

Building Our Husbands' Self-Esteem

Although this book deals mainly with the Christian woman's self-esteem, I must include the importance of our husbands' self-esteem. Low self-esteem is not a problem that only women have. Often the man who boasts and brags about himself to others is actually suffering from low self-esteem. Men's egos are very sensitive and require special attention from their wives.

I was recently at a ladies' seminar on courtship and marriage and I heard Foye Watkins say, "Ladies, if you want to be treated like a queen, you must treat your husband like a king." Jesus stated it another way in what we commonly call the Golden Rule: "Do unto others as you would have them do unto you."

We should daily seek to build up our husbands' self-esteem. They should feel their home is really their kingdom—a kingdom of peace and warmth and love. We should make their home one they are eager to come home to after work. Every wife should make her husband feel like he is the very best husband in the world.

How can we build our husbands' self-esteem? Below are some suggestions:

1. **Let your husband lead your family** (Ephesians 5:22-24). God gave our husbands this responsibility. He doesn't have to earn it. Being a submissive wife isn't an easy thing to do today because we are being told we should not submit. But God commanded it, and God knows what is best for us. We should express our confidence in our husband's ability to lead us and show that confidence by honoring his decisions. The "I told you so" or "You're making a mistake" attitude only destroys his self-esteem. We must pray for our husbands' abilities to lead us well.

2. **Learn to give praise and show appreciation.** When is the last time you told your husband how proud you are of him or told him how handsome he is? Men are no different from women in their need for praise. Have you told your husband you appreciate the way he provides for your family or the way he treats you? Why not write him a thank-you note for something special he has done?

Be careful to make your praise and signs of appreciation sincere. We should never use praise to manipulate our husbands and get our way.

3. **Don't nag!** Solomon gave us fair warning about nagging:

Proverbs 19:13
A foolish son is his father's ruin,
and a quarrelsome wife is like a constant dripping.

Proverbs 21:9
Better to live on a corner of the roof
than share a house with a quarrelsome wife.

It is easier to say "Don't nag" than practice it. Consider how you would feel if your husband constantly pointed out your faults or was always saying, "I wish you would...." I often wonder if nagging causes deafness. It seems the more women nag the less men hear. Be on your guard. We often nag without realizing it. It can become a bad habit. We need to replace nagging with praise.

4. **Accept your husband as he is.** Marabel Morgan gives four "A's" for wives in her book *The Total Woman.* They are "accept him, admire him, adapt to him, and appreciate him." The concept of acceptance is expressed in many other books as well. We are often guilty of trying to change our husbands and mold them into what we want them to be. Our husbands often resent this and feel rejected because we don't love them for themselves.

Make a list of qualities that caused you to fall in love with your husband. Make a list of his faults and throw them away. Dwelling on your husband's bad points affects your attitude toward him and damages his self-esteem.

5. **Be supportive of him.** Your husband wants to feel successful. He is much farther down the road to success if he knows he has your support. Wives can help their husbands become better businessmen, fishermen, fathers, church members or anything by continually expressing their confidence in them and pledging their support. If you have difficulty supporting your husband, find the wife of a successful man in your congregation and seek her advice. How has she helped her husband?

Conclusion

Our families affect our self-esteem more than any people on earth. In return, we have a tremendous influence in molding our family members' self-esteem. We must learn from our experiences as children. As adult Christian women we should continually strive to build the self-esteem of our parents, husbands, and children. As we serve others and build them up, our self-esteem will improve, because we are being useful. Our relationship with God is revealed in our relationships with others.

For Thought & Discussion

1. Make a list of things your parents did that helped you have a good self-esteem. Share them in a class discussion.

2. How can we help those who have come from a poor family background improve their self-esteem? Discuss various ways people have compensated.

3. Describe how the woman sets the emotional tone for her family. How does your family react to your different moods?

4. Give examples of how building our families' self-esteem is reciprocated.

5. Make a list of the five qualities you admire most in your husband. Take time to write him a note of praise and appreciation.

6. Discuss what it means to be a submissive wife. Find examples of Bible wives who were and were not submissive. How did this affect their husbands?

7. How do our husbands influence our self-esteem? How are we to respond if our husbands nag, point out our faults, or never show appreciation?

8. If you want "to be treated like a queen, treat your husband like a king." How can we make our husbands feel more like kings and make our homes more of a kingdom?

9

Good Family Relationships

PART 2: BUILDING SELF-ESTEEM IN CHILDREN

Other than our relationship with God, there is no greater influence on how we feel about ourselves than the home. We examined our early family backgrounds and our relationship with our husbands in Chapter 8. Because of the importance of early family background, I felt it was necessary to include a chapter on how we can build self-esteem in our children. The role we have as Christian mothers carries with it the responsibility of instilling in our children a sense of self-worth.

Let me begin by saying I am not an expert on building self-esteem in children. Parenting is a new experience for me and I have much to learn! (At the time of this writing I have one son, twenty months old and another baby is on the way.) The material I will include in this chapter comes from literature I have read, advice from successful parents, experiences in teaching school, and lessons from my own parents.

Is your child's self-esteem a reflection of your self-esteem? A young Christian mother once confided in me, "I have such a low self-esteem. I don't feel good about myself at all. The thing that concerns me most is that now my daughter is three. She already has a poor self-esteem. What can I do? I don't want her to feel like I do." This mother saw her self-esteem coming out in her daughter. It opened her eyes and made her realize that how she felt about herself was important. She had to work on improving her own self-esteem in order to improve her daughter's self-esteem.

We see this time and time again. Parents who have a high self-esteem are more likely to have children with high self-esteem. On the other hand, parents who lack confidence and a feeling of worth often pass these feelings on to their children. It doesn't mean they don't love their children or that they are bad parents. It just means self-esteem may be somewhat contagious. Perhaps before you examine how you can build your child's self-esteem, you need to examine your own. Do you want your child's self-esteem to be like yours?

Example! Example! Example!

Our homes provide the atmosphere in which a child's self-esteem is built. This is especially true during the preschool years of a child. Most of the research done on children's self-esteem has focused on experiences in the first three years of life. If a child feels loved, accepted and useful in early years, they will consider their home to be a haven when they begin school and their self-esteem is challenged. Rather than turning to outlets of escape such as drugs, alcohol and sex, they turn to home knowing they will find a sense of worth and warm acceptance.

Our example is so important in building a child's self-esteem. Our actions speak louder than words. We may tell a child, "I'm glad you're a part of our family," yet never spend time listening or playing with that child. This only causes confusion to a young child. We must live what we say. Our attitudes and actions toward ourselves, our family, the church and those outside the church have a tremendous effect on a child's attitude toward himself and others. Anne C. Bernstein wrote:

> *Children will come to value themselves as they have been valued by the significant people in their lives: treated with respect, they will respect themselves and be respectful to others in their turn... Children learn to treat themselves as they are treated — acceptance leads to self-acceptance, respect to self-respect, discipline to self-discipline, responsibility to self-reliance and cooperation.*
> (*Parents,* "Feeling Great (About Myself)," September 1982)

What kind of atmosphere are you providing for your family? Is it obvious to your children that God comes first and is the basis for your feelings toward self and others? Do they see a mother who is submissive and supportive of their father? Can they find security and calmness rather than confusion? Does love abound in actions as well as in words? Is respect, fairness, and discipline a part of that love? Is prayer a family practice as well as an individual one? How would your example be different if Jesus came to visit your home?

I remember seeing the following poem displayed in my orthodontist's office when I was in high school. I would read it each visit. It took on an entirely different meaning after I had a child of my own. I taped it to my refrigerator to constantly remind me of the importance of my example.

Children Learn What they Live

If a child lives with criticism . . . . *He learns to condemn*

If a child lives with hostility . . . . *He learns to fight*

If a child lives with ridicule . . . . *He learns to be shy*

If a child lives with shame . . . . *He learns to feel guilty*

If a child lives with tolerance . . . . *He learns to be patient*

If a child lives with encouragement . . . . *He learns confidence*

If a child lives with praise . . . . *He learns to appreciate*

If a child lives with fairness . . . . *He learns justice*

If a child lives with security . . . . *He learns to have faith*

If a child lives with approval . . . . *He learns to like himself*

If a child lives with acceptance and friendship
He learns to find love in the world

—DOROTHY LAW NOLTE

Jesus taught about the importance of our example in the Sermon on the Mount when He told His disciples, "You are the salt of the earth... You are the light of the world" (Matthew 5:13-16). Our light should shine its brightest in our own homes.

Proverbs 22:6 says, "Train up a child in the way he should go and when he is old he will not depart from it." We immediately think of training them by taking them to church and reading them Bible stories. I believe that training also includes a day-in and day-out example of godly living. Children won't depart from the training if they see it produces happy, useful lives that have purpose and meaning. Children need to know what they hear in church and Bible school is what they see at home. There is no room for hypocrisy. It all points back to our right relationship with God!

Strategies For Building Self-Esteem

Once we realize the importance of our role in building self-esteem in our children, how can we go about doing it? What are some specific things we can do?

Dr. James Dobson's book, *Hide Or Seek*, is devoted to the subject of how to build self-esteem in children. It is based on Christian principles and is an excellent resource for parents. I would highly recommend it for your church library as well as your personal library. Dr. Dobson devotes a large section of his book to strategies for esteem. We will briefly examine some of his suggestions.

1. **Examine the values in your own home.** The first step in building your child's self-esteem is to examine your own feelings toward that child. Are you secretly disappointed about the way your child looks or acts? Did you want a boy instead of a girl? Does the child represent a financial burden? Do you resent the freedom you lost or the demands the child places on your time?

Much of your child's self-esteem results from the way he thinks you see him. When a child is convinced he is greatly loved and respected by his parents, he is inclined to accept his own worth as a person. What a child sees mirrored in his parents' eyes eventually becomes his self-portrait. Research has shown that among families that encourage high self-esteem in children, the most common characteristic is total or near total acceptance of children by their parents. Parents value their children for who they are instead of what they do. Feeling loved helps a child to accept his deficiencies without damage to his self-esteem.

2. **Reserve adolescence for the adolescents.** After Jonathan was born I had so many mothers tell me, "Enjoy them while they're little. They don't stay young very long." How true! But parents, along with toy manufacturers and television, are pushing children right out of childhood and into an adolescent world.

Clep Shupp, in an article "Little Girls Are Too Sexy Too Soon," described ways in which mothers push their daughters into adolescence. She included such things as displaying a child's body in "cute" costumes for ballet or baton twirling, the early use of make-up, encouraging boyfriends at early ages, wearing bras before there is a need, and playing with Barbie dolls. All this leads to the trend for earlier dating and sexual awareness.

Parents need to screen the influences to which their children are exposed. Activities should be appropriate for each age. Let's don't make childhood extinct.

3. **Teach your child a "no-knock" policy.** A person who talks about his deficiencies and failures is usually telling you he has a low self-esteem. Constant self-criticism is a bad habit. It reminds us how we feel about ourselves and influences the way others feel toward us.

While children should not be taught to boast and brag, they also must learn not to talk about their flaws. Parents must be very careful about what they say about their children in front of others. Children are very sensitive and often judge themselves by what they hear their parents telling others. The "no-knock" policy should be practiced by the entire family.

4. **Help your child to compensate.** Let's face it! Not all children are beautiful, smart, athletic or talented. How do we prepare children to confront a world that highly values these things? We must teach them to compensate.

Compensation means a person counterbalances his weaknesses by capitalizing on his strengths. It is our job as parents to help our children find these strengths and learn to use them for all the self-satisfaction they will yield. Find something your child can do well and help him develop that skill. Help them realize their strengths at an early age. They will soon accept themselves with an attitude such as, "Maybe I'm not the best ball player in my class, but I can play the piano better than most."

5. **Help your child to compete.** Even though we may not agree with the values of the world, our children are forced to compete in the world. To help our children compete in a world where "beauty and brains are everything," we must teach them these values are temporal and unworthy. We must begin very early teaching the true values of life: devotion to God, love for all, kindness, integrity, trustworthiness, etc. A child who sees these values demonstrated at home is much better able to adjust and compete in a world outside his home.

6. **Discipline without damaging self-esteem.** Dr. Stanley Coopersmith studied the self-esteem of 1,738 normal middle-class boys and found the group of boys having the highest self-esteem came from homes where parents had been significantly more strict in their approach to discipline. The homes were also characterized by democracy and openness. Once boundaries for behavior were established, there was freedom for individual personalities to grow and develop.

The Bible advises us to discipline our children: "He who spares the rod hates his son, but he who loves him is careful to discipline him" (Proverbs 13:23). "Do not withhold discipline from a child; if you punish him with a rod he will not die. Punish him with the rod and save his soul from death" (Proverbs 23:13-14). A parent can damage a child's self-esteem by ridicule, disrespect, threats to withdraw love, abuse, and verbal rejection. Discipline must be administered with love and in such a manner that a child learns from the experience.

7. **Keep a close eye on the classroom.** Parents should stay informed about the educational progress of their children. Failure in school is one of the most devastating blows to a child's self-esteem. If your child is having difficulty in school, try to find out why. Most schools provide a testing service which can help pinpoint if your child is an underachiever (a child who refuses to use the ability he has), a slow learner, or has a learning disability.

If your child is a slow learner and does not have the ability to do well in school, de-emphasize academic achievement as a value in your home. Anything that your child cannot accomplish, despite his best efforts, should be toned down in importance. Try to maximize the educational potential of each child without sacrificing self-esteem. Expect each child to do his best, whatever that is. Be careful not to compare children's academic performance, because one child's best may be an "A" while another child's best work may only produce a "C." Know your child's abilities.

8. **Avoid overprotection and dependency.** I once saw an embroidered picture of two children sitting on a fence. Its caption was, "There are two things we must give our children. One is roots and the other is wings." While we must provide guidance for our children, we must also give them freedom and responsibility.

The best preparation for responsible adulthood comes from training in responsibility during childhood. Each age brings a gradual addition of responsibilities and the freedom to make certain decisions. "The parent must gain his freedom from the child so that the child can gain his freedom from his parents" (Dobson).

The overprotective mother does everything for her child and expects nothing in return. As a result, the child grows up thinking only of himself. He has difficulty making decisions and exercises very little self-discipline. Parents must love, teach and guide their children, but they must also help their children develop properly by teaching them the value of work and by being willing to "let go" at the appropriate times.

9. **Prepare for adolescence.** Lines of communication should be open throughout childhood. The generation gap that often occurs during teenage years usually begins early in childhood when parents are too busy to listen and talk. As a child approaches adolescence, it is very important that parents take the time to talk with their child and prepare them for the times ahead. The time spent may alleviate some of the fears, anxieties and discouragements that so often accompany adolescence.

Dr. Dobson recommends the following items be included in the discussions: physical changes, feelings of inferiority and confusion, peer pressure (conformity), identity formation, emotional and personality changes, sexual fascination and fear, and increasing independence. Many parents need to educate themselves on these topics before discussing them with their children.

Other Suggestions

The nine strategies listed above are by no means exhaustive of ways we can build our children's self-esteem. Below are some additional suggestions that Christian parents have given.

1. **Begin very early training your child about God.** If the most important influence on an adult's self-esteem is a right relationship with God, we should help our children develop that relationship. A church elder once said, "You had better mold them while you can hold them." A child is never too young to learn of God's love. I am so amazed at what infants learn in a cradle roll class at church. If children learn what God's love means and learn to love God, the Bible, and others in return, their self-esteem has a great advantage.

2. **Spend time with your children.** We would probably be amazed at how little time we spend with our children if we sat down and totaled the minutes. I am referring to quality time in actual talking, listening, playing, studying and working together. It does not include time in front of a television.

One young man said, "My father was a great dad, but he was always so busy. I was always jealous of the guys whose dads came to watch them play ball or took them fishing." What better gift could we give our children than our time and our support in their activities?

3. **Learn to give praise and encouragement.** Children can recognize empty, insincere praise. Praise should not be given just for the sake of praise. On the other hand, children need to know their parents are proud of them. Praising their accomplishments may help them through hard times and give them the self-confidence to tackle difficult tasks.

4. **Pray for each child each day by name.** This practice may not directly affect your child's self-esteem, but it can give you confidence as a parent. You know God has a part in molding your children and you have asked for His divine guidance.

5. **Make your child feel useful.** A big part of self-worth is feeling needed and useful. Even small children should be taught the value of work by giving them chores to do. Make them responsible and help them understand a family functions best when each member carries out his responsibilities.

I received "A Child's Ten Commandments" listed below in a ladies' class several years ago. I do not know the author but I felt it was appropriate to our discussion.

a Child's ten Commandments to parents

1. *My hands are small; please con't expect perfection whenever I make a bed, draw a picture, or throw a ball. My legs are short, please slow down so that I can keep up with you.*

2. *My eyes have not seen the world as yours have; please let me explore safely; don't restrict me unnecessarily.*

3. *Housework will always be there. I'm only little for such a short time — please take time to explain things to me about this wonderful world, and do so willingly.*

4. *My feelings are tender; please be sensitive to my needs; don't nag me all day long. (You wouldn't want to be nagged for your inquisitiveness.) Treat me as you would like to be treated.*

5. *I am a special gift from God; please treasure me as God intended you to do, holding me accountable for my actions, giving me guidelines to live by, and disciplining me in a loving manner.*

6. *I need your encouragement. Please go easy on the criticism; remember, you can criticize the things I do without criticizing me.*

7. *Please give me the freedom to make decisions concerning myself. Permit me to fail, so that I can learn from my mistakes. Then someday I'll be prepared to make the kind of decisions life requires of me.*

8. *Please don't do things for me. Somehow that makes me feel that my efforts didn't quite measure up to your expectations. I know it's hard, but please don't try to compare me with my brother and my sister.*

9. *Please don't be afraid to leave for a weekend together. Kids need vacations from parents, just as parents need vacations from kids. Besides, it's a great way to show us kids that your marriage is very special.*

10. *Please take me to Sunday school and church regularly, setting a good example for me to follow. I enjoy learning more about God.*

Conclusion

"Heavenly Father, the privilege and responsibility of being a mother demands so much. Please give me wisdom and guidance as I try to be a good mother. May my example be godly. Help me to train my children to love You, Your Word, and to be useful servants. Help me and my children to grow in our self-esteem as we grow in Your love. Help us to center our homes and our individual lives around You. Thank you, God, for accepting and loving us even when we were unlovable. In Jesus' name, Amen."

For Thought & Discussion

1. How do our children's abilities affect our personal self-esteem? Should we allow our children's achievements to boost our self-esteem and their failures destroy it?

2. Ask the teenagers of your congregation to rate their self-esteem on a scale from one to ten. Then ask them to list some things parents can do to build their self-esteem. Share your findings in class.

3. Describe some events in these Bible characters' lives that could have influenced their self-esteem: Jacob and Esau; Rachel and Leah; Moses; David; Timothy. (For example, Joseph received the beautiful coat from his father, yet was ridiculed by his brothers.)

4. Divide the class into small groups and have each group discuss a different strategy for building self-esteem in depth. Allow some time for each group to briefly report to the class.

5. What are some specific household chores that are appropriate for various ages? How can these chores teach responsibility and make a child feel useful?

6. Which of the "Child's Ten Commandments To Parents" would your child have written? Make a commitment to work on that specific area during the next week.

7. Make a list of your child's strengths and best abilities. How can you help him develop skills in those areas? Examine how you react when your child does poorly at something. How can you offer more encouragement?

8. How does our example in the following areas affect our children's self-esteem: self-criticism; church involvement; service to others; critical attitudes; personal accomplishments?

10

Praise & Encouragement From Others

The last four chapters have discussed how we can build our self-esteem through a right relationship with God and with our family. Hopefully, as we study these lessons on self-esteem builders we will grow in our personal self-esteem and also learn how to build the self-esteem of others. We should always be well-equipped to help others and build them up.

According to our survey, praise and encouragement from others was the third most significant influence in building a good self-esteem. Does it surprise you that the three greatest self-esteem builders in Christian women involve relationships with God, family, and others outside our family? For the Christian, self-esteem is not based on beauty, intelligence, or wealth. Instead, it is based on the bonds found in relationships. These are bonds of love, peace, acceptance and feeling needed. The bonds begin in our relationship to God and extend into our homes and then into other relationships.

Praise and encouragement from others is especially found in our relationship with other Christians. Thirty-seven percent of the women surveyed said their Christian friends were among the people who have contributed the most to helping them build a good self-esteem. Twenty-seven percent said Christian friends had a greater influence than even their parents or their husband. Does that say something about the need for strong relationships in the church? It should! Our ability to establish ties and friendships with our Christian family has a significant effect on our self-esteem.

It is becoming easy to see why those who have a difficult time getting along with others often have a poor self-esteem. Their inability to establish worthwhile relationships causes them to think less of themselves. Those who have the ability to get along with others and who form strong ties and friendships have someone to turn to when things go wrong or when their self-esteem is threatened. They seek encouragement and find it.

I am convinced that one reason God gave us the church was so Christians wouldn't have to be alone. God knew that we need one another! Hebrews 10:24-25 is a familiar scripture we use to teach that we are not to forsake the assemblies, but we often overlook the part of those verses that tells us *why* we are to assemble. One of the purposes of the church's meeting together is to "spur one another on toward love and good deeds" and "to encourage one another."

Praise and encouragement are not self-esteem builders because they give us a "big head." God knew we needed to receive praise and encouragement, and the church is one place where we can find it. Paul began the majority of his epistles with words of praise and encouragement. Take time to read the first few verses of Romans, Corinthians, Philippians, Thessalonians, Timothy, Colossians and Philemon and note how Paul praises and encourages these Christians. It must have been easier to listen to his rebukes after hearing his praise, thanksgiving and love for them. What a joy it must have been to hear Paul's words of encouragement. Those same words are recorded in the Bible and offer us encouragement today.

Barnabas is another example of a great encourager whom God used. His name even means "Son of Encouragement" (Acts 4:36). It was Barnabas who took Saul to the apostles after Saul was baptized (Acts 9:27), and he encouraged him during his days as a young Christian. We read of Barnabas again in Acts 11:22-23 and Acts 14:22 as he encourages Christians to be true to the faith. We need more encouragers like Barnabas today. God desires that Christians find praise and encouragement from other Christians. He knows the strength it gives us in facing the world. We must know how to give praise and encouragement to others as well as how to receive it.

How To Accept Praise & Encouragement

There are many Christians who have never benefited from praise and encouragement from others because they have never learned to accept it. How many times has someone paid you a compliment such as, "You really look nice today," and you responded with, "My, this dress is so old and my hair wouldn't do a thing this morning." The person who paid you the compliment could care less about how old your dress is. They were sincerely praising you. A simple response of, "Thank you, I appreciate that," would be much more appropriate.

Have you ever felt ill and had someone call and ask if they could help you in some way? Usually we reply, "Thank you, but we'll make it just fine." Deep inside you are probably thinking, "If someone could just take the kids so I could get some rest, or if someone could go to the grocery store and pick up a few things for me...." Someone offered but you turned them down. We turn down too many offers for encouragement and help because we don't like to admit that we need help. Our pride gets in the way.

I used to be like this until I heard a lesson on encouragement at a ladies' Bible study. The Christian sister who presented the lesson made the statement, "When you reject praise, encouragement or help from another Christian, you are not only hurting yourself but also that other Christian. You are denying them the privilege of giving and serving, and those are important elements of Christian growth." I had never stopped to think of it from that point of view. Since then I have tried to swallow my pride and accept others' encouragement, praise and help.

Just this week a Christian sister called and offered to keep Jonathan one afternoon so I could work on this chapter. My first impulse was to say, "No, thank you. You're so busy and I can work on it during Jonathan's naptime." But I took her up on her offer. It gave me a chance to study and prepare the contents in this chapter. That encouraged me tremendously. We must learn to graciously accept praise and encouragement from others and learn from it.

Jesus knew how to accept praise and encouragement. Three gospels record the account of Mary breaking the alabaster box of expensive perfume on Jesus' head (Matthew 26:6-13; Mark 14:3-9; John 12:2-8). Mary was demonstrating affection and love for Jesus through this act. This must have been a great encouragement to Jesus. Imagine how Mary might have felt if Jesus had denied her this privilege. Instead he said, "Wherever this gospel is preached throughout the world, what she has done will also be told, in the memory of her." Both Mary and Jesus benefited from this act.

Some Christians give and give to others but never learn the joy of receiving. We should never become so selfish that we only expect to receive. On the other hand, we should allow others the joy of giving by learning to gratefully and graciously accept praise and encouragement.

You may be thinking, "My problem is that no one offers me any praise or encouragement. I would gladly accept it if they did." If that is your case, let me make a few suggestions.

1. **Turn to God's Word for encouragement.** The Bible is a constant source of encouragement available to us at all times. Open it and read it. The Psalms remind us of God' love, care and faithfulness. The Gospels make us aware of Jesus' love and also His earthly struggles. Passages such as Romans 8 and Philippians 4 are favorites of many Christians because of the encouragement they offer. Everyone can find encouragement in the Bible if he will only look.

2. **Find encouragement in the lives of others.** Paul told Philemon, "Your love has given me great joy and encouragement, because you, brother, have refreshed the hearts of the saints" (Philemon verse 7). Philemon didn't directly encourage Paul, but his love for others had indirectly encouraged Paul. Watch the lives of other Christians and see if you can't find encouragement.

I am encouraged every time I see a Chrisitan wife come to church alone even though her husband pressures her to stay home. It encourages me to see young people maturing in Christ and remaining faithful to the church. A new Christian's zeal and desire for growth also encourages me. There are many examples. Remember, sometimes encouragement comes indirectly.

3. **Form a few very strong relationships.** Even in a family, we are naturally closer to some than others. Jesus was closer to Peter, James and John than the other apostles. We need a few very special friends whom we know we can laugh and cry with and call on at any time if we need help.

If you don't have such a relationship, you may have to initiate one. Tell someone you would like to get to know them better and grow closer. Realize that relationships take time. As you spend time with people you will learn how to praise and encourage them, and they will do the same for you. Don't be afraid to get close to people.

4. **Learn to ask for encouragement.** Many times our Christian family would gladly help us, but they aren't aware of our needs. Sometimes we have to openly tell someone, "I need your help and encouragement." I recently attended a home Bible study where each Christian lady was asked to share some area of her life where she felt encouragement was needed. Some said they needed encouragement in daily Bible study, or being more submissive or being a better parent. Then we prayed about it and promised one another to be more diligent in our encouragement.

Once people are aware of our needs, they are usually more than willing to help. If you need encouragement, tell someone. Don't hide your needs. Jesus said, "Ask and it will be given to you" (Matthew 7:7).

How To Give Praise & Encouragement

When we receive praise and encouragement from others it helps our self-esteem because we know others care. Our self-esteem also improves when we learn how to give praise and encouragement. It takes the attention off ourselves and focuses it on others. Paul told the Philippians to not just look at their own interests, but also to the interests of others (Philippians 2:4).

There are many scriptures that teach the necessity of praising and encouraging one another. Consider the following:

An anxious heart weighs a man down, but a kind word cheers him up.
(Proverbs 12:25)

A man finds joy in giving an apt reply—and how good is a timely word.
(Proverbs 15:25)

Bear one another's burdens, and so fulfill the law of Christ.
(Galatians 6:2)

...Warn those who are idle, encourage the timid, help the weak, be patient with everyone.
(I Thessalonians 5:14)

Dear children, let us not love with words or tongue but with actions and in truth.
(I John 3:18)

86

Much of the praise and encouragement we give to others is done verbally. What is said and how we say it is so important! The last scripture, I John 3:18, teaches us that our actions also demonstrate praise, encouragement, and love. Our words and actions must come from an unselfish heart and a genuine love for others.

How can we become more like Barnabas? How can we improve our ability to praise and encourage others? It comes by developing an attitude of giving and continually looking for ways to give. Jesus taught, "Give, and it will be given to you. A good measure, pressed down, shaken together and running over, will be poured into your lap. For with the measure you use, it will be measured to you" (Luke 6:38). What kind of measure are you using? What are you giving to others?

Ron Willingham devoted a chapter of his women's Bible course, *Love, Joy, Peace,* to gift giving. He describes three kinds of gifts: word gifts, time gifts, and gift gifts. Each of these types of gifts are appropriate ways to give praise and encouragement.

1. **Word gifts.** A word gift is something nice you say to another person. It is one of the most powerful things we can do to help someone like themselves. Most people crave word gifts. A word gift can be a compliment, a cheerful greeting, an expression of gratitude, a statement of praise, or an expression of love. A word gift may even be passing on a compliment you heard someone give. ("I heard someone say that you are an excellent cook.") Word gifts may be given verbally or written in a note or card.

Word gifts come most easily for those who are positive and seeking good in others. They must be given sincerely. Sometimes the best word gift we can give someone is to say, "I'm praying for you." Prayer is a gift itself. What greater way could we encourage someone than to let them know we are praying for them?

2. **Time gifts.** Time gifts are units of our time that we give to someone. They may be the most valuable gifts we can give. Time gifts are given when we visit someone who is lonely or ill, call someone who needs encouragement, invite a newcomer into our home, keep someone's children, or listen to someone who has a problem. When we give someone our time we are telling them they are important to us. We must never allow ourselves to become so busy that we cannot take time for others. Money and gift gifts will never replace the value of the gift of our time.

3. **Gift gifts.** Gift gifts are things we make or purchase to give someone. They don't have to cost much. Some of the most meaningful gifts are inexpensive — a single flower (maybe even one you've grown in your yard), a card, a box of stationery, someone's favorite candy bar, some home-baked treat, and on and on.

Last week my son received a stick of gum in the mail from his grandparents. You would have thought it was the most expensive toy in the world because he was so thrilled. The thought often means more than the actual gift.

Handmade gifts or food that has been prepared are very special gift gifts because they are also time gifts. The time involved in preparing them says, "You are special!" An elder's wife took watermelon to a Christian sister because she knew the sister loved watermelon. The thing that made it so special was the fact that the elder's wife had cut the watermelon into pieces and removed the seeds. What a gift of love!

If you have never been one to give praise and encouragement to others, begin today. If you are shy or it seems awkward, begin slowly. Set yourself some goals regarding who you would like to praise and encourage and how you can do it. If you do it often enough, it will soon become a habit and flow naturally. You never know the effect you may have on someone's self-esteem — not to mention your own. The Bible teaches that those who give the most will receive the most (II Corinthians 9:6; Proverbs 11:24; Luke 6:38; Acts 20:35).

your Life Will Be Richer If—

ON THIS DAY: YOU WILL MAKE AN EFFORT TO—
Mend a quarrel,
Search for a forgotten friend.
Dismiss a suspicion and replace it with trust.
Write a letter to someone who misses you.
Encourage someone who has lost faith.
Keep a promise.
Forget an old grudge.
Examine your demands on others and vow to reduce them.
Fight for a principle.
Express your gratitude.

Overcome an old fear
Take two minutes to appreciate the beauty of nature.
Tell someone you love him.
Tell him again.
And again.
And again.   —AUTHOR UNKNOWN

Barriers That Hinder Us

Christians must be on guard against barriers that hinder us from giving or receiving praise and encouragement. One barrier is **selfishness**. The selfish person is one who always expects to receive praise and encouragement and becomes offended when she doesn't. Her feelings are easily hurt, and she is prone to criticize others. The selfish person is also one who becomes so involved in her own job, family and activities that she "just doesn't have time" to encourage others or develop relationshps with those outside her own circle.

Another barrier is **superficiality**. These people never get past the "acquaintance stage" in their relationships. Their relationships lack depth and openness. Some don't want to be open because they may be afraid others won't like them or they may betray a confidence. The superficial person may freely praise others, but they lack the depth to really know how to encourage others and express their need for encouragement.

A third barrier is **pride**. We mentioned this earlier. Pride keeps us from admitting when we need encouragement and accepting praise or help from others. It also causes us to compare ourselves to others.

Jealousy is another barrier. We may deliberately withhold praise from someone because we are jealous of them. We may not offer encouragement because we feel that someone already gets more encouragement than we do.

These barriers come from within our hearts. They may be "quiet sins" because they are hidden from others. We must never allow Satan to creep in and use these barriers on us. They will only harden our hearts and make us unwilling to give or receive praise and encouragement from others.

Conclusion

A good self-esteem is built around worthwhile relationships with God, our family, and others. A big part of these relationships is knowing we can find praise and encouragement through them. These are relationships where people know our faults and weaknesses but love us anyway.

Self-esteem is built as we receive praise and encouragement from others. It is also built as we give praise and encouragement. The church is God's family. Praise and encouragement should be a daily practice among that family. Not only will it help our self-esteem, but it allows us to boost the self-esteem of our brothers and sisters in Christ.

For Thought & Discussion

1. Have the members of the class share some specific ways people have encouraged them. Make a list of the different ways we can encourage others.

2. Divide your class into groups of five or six. Share word gifts. Have each member of the group praise or encourage one member of your group. Go around until all members have received word gifts. Discuss how it felt to receive praise.

3. Write down the names of three people you plan to encourage within the next week. Beside their names, write how you plan to encourage them.

4. Read Hebrews 10:24-25. Discuss how we can make our worship services a greater source of encouragement.

5. Philemon's love for others indirectly encouraged Paul. Who are some people that indirectly have encouraged you?

6. Have members of the class share some scriptures that encourage them. Write the scriptures on a poster.

7. Compare the effects of praise and encouragement on your self-esteem with the effect of criticism.

8. Share some things that help develop strong, open relationships among Christian sisters.

11

Acceptance & Security

We have been discussing influences that help build a good self-esteem. Based on our survey, the six most significant influences are (1) a good relationship with God, (2) early family background, (3) praise and encouragement from others, (4) present family situation, (5) intelligence, competence, and education, and (6) acceptance and security. We included a discussion of our present family situation in chapters eight and nine. We will not include a chapter on intelligence, competence and education; however, your class may wish to discuss how these things affect our self-esteem.

We will devote an entire chapter to acceptance and security because of the role the church plays in this self-esteem builder. The opposite of acceptance, rejection, was listed by twelve percent of the women surveyed as the number one self-esteem destroyer. There is a definite need for people to know they fit in and to feel needed and loved.

This is one of the beauties of Christ's church. Think of your congregation and all the different types of people who compose it. There are different races, socioeconomic levels, educational backgrounds, family backgrounds, occupations, hobbies, talents, etc. Yet in the church we are all one family. We are all Christians, and we accept one another and love one another as a family would love each other. Jesus said this is how the world would know that we are His disciples (John 13:34-35). I doubt I would know very many members of our congregation if I were not a Christian, because we would not have much in common to draw us together. But because of God's love for us and our obedience to Him, we have everything in common.

Paul paints a beautiful picture of the church in Romans 12:4-8 and I Corinthians 12:12-27 when he described the church as a body. Each Christian is unique and has a unique role to play in the body, but all the members work together and help the body function at its best (Ephesians 4:16). For members to work together in unity we must have a spirit of acceptance. All parts of the body must feel secure and accepted and feel they are needed and vital to the body's function.

This acceptance and security cannot be found outside the church. Many have sought to find it in their jobs, civic clubs, community activities and even cults, but all of these things lack the basic ingredient of real internal acceptance and security — God's love. Because God has accepted us, we are secure in His love and we can accept one another. This security and acceptance builds our self-esteem. We know we have a place where we fit in, and we know we are needed in the church.

Acceptance

In building our self-esteem, acceptance becomes a two-way street. We must feel that we are accepted and needed, but we must also be willing to open our lives and accept others. You may feel that you are well accepted, but it is hard to feel good about yourself if you are not accepting others or if you are harboring feelings of dislike or jealousy.

Some people become so secure in their acceptance by a circle of close friends that they become cliquish and exclude others. We are taught in James 2:1-9 that we are to demonstrate acceptance to all. Rich or poor, black or white, young or old — in the church we are to be accepted and treated equally. There should be no favoritism shown among God's family.

The commands given in Romans 12:9-21 can certainly be applied in demonstrating our acceptance toward others. It involves sharing, practicing hospitality, praying, rejoicing and weeping together, being devoted to one another, and living in harmony with one another. Let us examine four groups of people who need to find acceptance in the church.

1. **Accept yourself.** We cannot feel like others have accepted us unless we first accept ourselves. Jesus taught the second greatest commandment is to love your neighbor as yourself (Matthew 22:39). How much do you love yourself? If you don't love yourself, chances are you have a difficult time loving others. This love for self is not to be vain conceit or pride in our lives. A true love for self goes back to our relationship with God as we talked about it in chapters six and seven. We can love and accept ourselves because of what God has done for us.

If you have a difficult time accepting yourself, sit down and analyze your life and your circumstances. What are the things that make it difficult for you to accept yourself? Write them down. Now look at the list and put a star by the things you can change. Make a commitment to change them. Then look at the things you cannot change. Stop and pray that God will help you accept those circumstances, be content (Philippians 4:11), and do the very best you can.

Many cannot accept themselves because they are too busy comparing themselves with others. They have a feeling of inferiority because someone else always looks better, has more money, is more talented, or any number of things. We must learn not to compare ourselves. Remember, Christians are all different and make up different parts of the body. God did not intend for us all to be alike. He made each Christian unique and special and has set aside a specific role for us in His body, the church, based upon our abilities and talents.

It is not how talented we are that matters. It is how we use our talent. Jesus' parable of the talents is recorded in Matthew 25:14-30 and Luke 19:11-27. Read the parable and analyze your talents. Are you using the ability God gave you, or are you hiding it because you feel inferior or because you won't accept yourself?

There is a popular plaque that says, "What you are is God's gift to you. What you become is your gift to God." What kind of gift are you presenting to God? Write down your specific talents and qualities you like about yourself. You may include things such as singing, teaching, sewing, cooking, needlework, ability to draw or paint, organization skills, typing, love for children, ability to meet people, ability to write, good housekeeping, love for reading, and on and on. Beside each item you list, write how you are using that talent for God's glory.

If you see that you are not using your abilities, find something to do. Ask someone or volunteer your help. The church is always in need of Bible teachers. If you do not have the ability to teach, perhaps you could help organize and keep up a supply room for teachers or fix bulletin boards. Does your congregation have a clothing or benevolence room that needs attending? Can you visit the ill, shut-ins, newcomers, or weak members and take food? Who fixes communion for your congregation? Is there someone who would enjoy being read to or could use your assistance in typing? Can you keep someone's children so they can visit? There is a job for everyone to do in the Lord's church if we are willing to recognize our talents and use them.

> *If you can't be a pine on the top of the hill,*
> *Be a shrub in the valley—but be*
> *The best little shrub at the side of the rill:*
> *Be a bush if you can't be a tree.*
> *If you can't be a bush, be a bit of the grass,*
> *Some highway to happier make;*
> *If you can't be a muskie, then just be a bass*
> *But the liveliest bass in the lake.*
> *We can't all be captains, we've got to be crew,*
> *There's something for all of us here;*
> *There's big work to do and there's lesser to do,*
> *And the task we must do is the near.*
> *If you can't be a highway, then just be a trail;*
> *If you can't be a sun, be a star.*
> *It isn't by size that you win or you fail—*
> *BE THE BEST OF WHATEVER YOU ARE.*
>
> —Douglas Wallock

If we recognize our talents and abilities and use them in the church we are going to feel more accepted by those in the church. Being involved helps us feel useful and needed. In return it helps us feel accepted. It then becomes easier to accept others and help them feel needed. Acceptance begins by accepting yourself.

2. **Accept new Christians.** Usually someone spends a great deal of time in teaching the gospel to a friend who is not a Christian. When they are baptized, there is much rejoicing and people rush to greet them. Then what happens? As time passes on, we give the new Christian less and less attention. The Bible studies may stop, and we often begin to expect instant maturity. If we are not careful, we will sit back in a few months and wonder why the new Christian isn't faithful. We lose so many new converts because we do not adequately accept them and give them the attention they need.

Lydia Shermon wrote a bulletin article entitled, "The Dilemma of the New Christian" in which she describes six needs of new Christians. By meeting these needs, new Christians are much more likely to remain faithful and develop into strong, mature Christians. The six needs are discussed briefly below:

A new Christian...

1. **NEEDS LOVE** in order to grow spiritually. A new Christian is more likely to change bad behavior and take interest in the church if he is praised often and shown love by the members. Peter compares new Christians to babies (I Peter 2:2-3). Think of how much attention a new baby requires. Babies need that attention for several years. A new Christian should be treated like a new baby.

2. **NEEDS TO FILL A GAP** once filled by worldly friends and activities. Leaving this gap gives Satan a better chance to win them back. New Christians need to be visited often or invited into homes of older members. They need to feel new friendships developing and have someone to turn to when they are tempted or discouraged.

3. **NEEDS ENCOURAGEMENT.** The best time to get a Christian involved in the church is immediately after his baptism. It is then he is usually most zealous. They need encouragement and praise for their efforts. Criticism or careless remarks may devastate a new Christian. We should give them positive attention at every opportunity.

4. **NEEDS EXAMPLES OF OLDER CHRISTIANS.** It is difficult to keep a new Christian zealous and involved if he looks around and sees that many of the older members are not working. Isn't it sad to think we may discourage a new Christian by our lack of zeal, concern or involvement?

5. **NEEDS CONTINUAL SPIRITUAL TEACHING.** Just because a person is baptized does not mean he knows everything in the Bible. There are still many fundamentals that may need to be taught (for example, instrumental music, the Lord's Supper, functions of the elders and deacons, etc.). Personal Bible studies should be continued for new Christians. Older members should help new members grow in their knowledge.

6. **NEEDS GROUP FELLOWSHIP.** New members need many opportunities to get to know other Christians and feel like they are accepted by them. Singings, parties, fellowship meals, sports, group Bible studies, etc., are excellent ways to get to know new Christians and draw them into the "family." The more attention and care new Christians receive, the more accepted they feel.

We have a responsibility to our new brothers and sisters in Christ. Our willingness to accept them and love them helps them to grow and also strengthens us.

3. **Accept newcomers.** The first few weeks after a family moves to a new community may be crucial to their spiritual development. If they go several weeks without meeting Christians or regularly attending services, they may gradually fall away from the church. On the other hand, if they immediately are visited and made to feel welcome and accepted, they may become more involved in the Lord's work than ever before. (Remember, we said earlier that getting involved helps us feel accepted.) I realize that newcomers have a responsibility to attend services and make themselves known. Often we don't know when Christians have moved into the community. We don't intentionally neglect them, we just aren't aware they are there.

There are some specific things we can do to help newcomers feel accepted and make their move and adjustment easier. First of all, look for new faces and visitors at all church services and make a point to meet them. Try to introduce them to some other church members. You may even ask them to sit with you during services. Sitting alone feels awkward and cold. We must be careful that we do not sit in the same spot and by the same people at every service. This may make a congregation appear cliquish and keep us from getting to meet the visitors. Some congregations recognize newcomers and visitors by having them wear a flower or a visitor's badge.

It helps if a congregation knows in advance that a family is moving to their area. Military families do this through the "AMEN" program. If you know you are moving, you may wish to write a congregation and inquire about their work and services before you move or have your elders write a letter introducing you to elders of another congregation. Christians are able to offer immediate help if they know you are coming. They may be there to help you unpack, bring you food, keep your children, give you a ride to services, recommend doctors or stores, or offer other gestures that immediately show you that you are welcome and accepted because you are a Christian.

I shall never forget the day we moved from Tuscaloosa, Alabama to Montgomery. It was so hard to leave Christian friends in Tuscaloosa. Just a few minutes after we arrived in Montgomery, a car pulled up and a lady said, "Don't worry about supper tonight. Some members from the Lakewood congregation are bringing food to you." What wonderful news! The following day the preacher came by to visit and a Christian sister came and helped unpack kitchen supplies. We were invited to a church picnic and we received so many invitations to visit in people's homes. We were overwhelmed with love and kindness. How could we help but feel accepted! There are many adjustments associated with a move. Quickly becoming involved with a Christian family makes the adjustments much easier.

4. **Accept those outside your age group.** Congregations today tend to segregate their members by age groups. We have youth ministers and activities for teenagers, a singles' group, a young marrieds' group, an adult group, and a senior citizens' group. There is nothing wrong with these groups because age groups have a lot in common; however, we should not become so involved in our age groups that we exclude other ages. Many teenagers in our congregation don't know the names of most older members because their activities are exclusively for teenagers.

Every age group needs all the other age groups to have a unified congregation. Older women are to teach the younger women and train them (Titus 2:3-5). On the other hand, the enthusiasm of youth can add so much to an older person's life. Young mothers need older women to counsel them on child rearing and to sometimes be substitute grandparents. They also need teenagers to babysit or help them tend to the children during church services. Elderly members may need younger members to cut their grass or make repairs in their homes.

We all need each other in special ways. There are so many things we can learn from one another and do for one another. Whether young or old, rich or poor, we are all one family in Christ. God has accepted us all; therefore, we should accept one another. It will help our self-esteem.

Security

Children like to feel secure. Many find their security in a blanket, a stuffed animal, a thumb, or favorite toy. One toy manufacturer has even come out with a security bunny. As children grow older they usually lay aside these physical things and find security in the love of their family and friends.

Adults are like children in their need to feel secure. Although adults don't suck their thumb and carry a blanket as Linus does, they often try to find security in jobs, money, and material possessions. None of these things provides real security because they are all temporal and earthly. Many adults have seen their self-esteem crumple when they have lost a job, gone through divorce, or financial difficulties. Their sense of security is gone.

A Christian can face difficult times and still feel secure and maintain a high self-esteem. The difference is that a Christian's security is found in God's love and grace. Romans 8 is like the security blanket for Christians. Read the entire chapter and see if it doesn't boost your confidence. It is so wonderful to know God works everything for our good (verse 28). He is always for us (verse 31). We can never be separated from God's love (verse 35). Through God, we are more than conquerors (verse 37). Now that is *real* security!!

Once again, self-esteem goes back to our relationship with God. Who can help feeling good about themselves when they know God is in control and working things out for their good?

Conclusion

Acceptance and security are important self-esteem builders. Women need to feel that other people accept them and that they fit in. To feel accepted, Christian women should become involved in the Lord's work. We must also be willing to demonstrate acceptance to others.

Real security is found in God's love. As our faith grows, so will our security and our self-esteem.

For Thought & Discussion

▦ 1. Have class members share some experiences associated with their moves. How have congregations made the adjustment of moving easier?

▦ 2. How did Barnabas help Paul when Paul was a new Christian? (Acts 9:26-30) Make a list of new Christians in your congregation (baptized within the last year). What is being done or can be done to help them grow spiritually?

▦ 3. What can be done to promote more interaction between various age groups? List some specific activities. Choose one activity and take it on as a class project.

▦ 4. Divide the class into small groups. Have each member share a talent they possess. Discuss how these talents can be used in the Lord's work.

▦ 5. While in small groups, have each member share how they came to know Christ and the changes it made in their lives. What made them feel accepted and secure as young Christians?

▦ 6. Make a poster comparing a Christian's source of security with the world's sources of security.

▦ 7. Make a list of hymns and/or scriptures that give us a feeling of security in God.

12

Self-Discipline

The last six chapters have discussed the influences that Christian women feel build their self-esteem. Even though self-discipline was not listed as a choice on our survey, I feel a great need to include a chapter on it. The more I study self-esteem and observe women, the more I see the importance of self-discipline in developing a good self-esteem.

Self-discipline (or self-control) isn't something that some of us are born with and others are not. It must be learned and cultivated. Paul told Timothy, "For God did not give us a spirit of timidity, but a spirit of power, of love and of self-discipline" (II Timothy 2:7). Just as God has given every Christian the ability to love, He has also given us the ability to be self-disciplined. He has planted the seed in our lives, but each of us must do our part to make the seed grow and blossom.

Solomon said the woman Folly is loud, undisciplined and without knowledge in Proverbs 9:13. (I often wonder why Folly is referred to as a woman. Was Solomon trying to tell us ladies something?) Are you undisciplined like the woman Folly? Here are some questions that may help you decide:

1. Do you get up as soon as the alarm goes off?

2. Do you have a set time for prayer and Bible study each day?

3. Are you consistently late?

4. Do you pick up your clothes whenever you take them off?

5. Do you procrastinate?

6. Do you become frustrated because you can't seem to accomplish all the things that need to be done?

7. Do your good intentions usually get accomplished?

8. Do you try to look nice and take pride in your appearance each day?

9. Are you organized? Does your house, your work, and your time reflect organization?

10. Do you react on impulse or do you plan ahead?

If you consider yourself to be an undisciplined person, don't blame anyone but yourself. Remember, we're talking about **self**-discipline. Get ready to change. You will feel so much better about yourself, and you will be able to accomplish so much more.

If you consider yourself to be disciplined, please, share your secrets with your Christian sisters. You will be doing your undisciplined sister a great favor, and she will love you for your help. There is not one big secret to self-discipline. What works for one woman may not work for another, but your secret will probably help someone.

Why is self-discipline important? How does it affect our self-esteem? Self-discipline will influence how our time is spent, how we control our moods and feelings, how we look, and what we accomplish in our lifetimes. An undisciplined woman may have a poor self-esteem because she stays frustrated and feels like she never really accomplishes anything worthwhile. She is full of good intentions that never get done and she may become angry with herself because she knows she should do better.

On the other hand, a disciplined woman may have a higher self-esteem because she has a purpose for each day, and she feels good when she knows she accomplished what she set out to do. She has more time for herself and for God because she has organized her time and set priorities in her life. The disciplined woman is usually a very busy woman. When something needs to be done at church, the busiest people are usually the ones asked to do it. Why? People have learned that those who are busiest are usually the most disciplined, and they accomplish what they set out to do.

What makes a person disciplined? Why are some more disciplined than others? There are so many little things that can contribute to self-discipline, but I want us to consider three in this chapter. Those three are: organization; goals; and time management.

Organization

One day I was watching *Sesame Street* with Jonathan. On the show Bert and Ernie (puppets) were busy trying to put their toys away. Ernie got all the large toys while Bert put away the small ones. They repeated the skit, only this time they put the toys away by colors. I thought to myself, "If Bert and Ernie can get organized, why can't we adults?"

Anne Ortlund, in her book *Disciplines of the Beautiful Woman*, gives some of the most practical suggestions for organizing your life that I have ever found. (Every Christian woman would benefit by having a copy of that book in her personal library!) I want to share three of her suggestions:

1. **Reshape your life into priorities.** What are the most important things in your life? Write them down and consider why they are important. These priorities will greatly influence your personal goals and how you organize your time. Do your top priorities include God, the church, and the lost?

The Marriage Enrichment Film Series by Paul Faulkner and Carl Brecheen uses an expression that really hit home with me. It is, "We neglect the important to tend to the urgent." Isn't that true? We become so busy tending to the things that must be done immediately that we don't even realize we are neglecting the really important things in life.

We should continually remind ourselves of what the priorities in our lives are and evaluate our time and lifestyles to see if they reflect those priorities.

2. **Learn to "eliminate and concentrate."** These words can apply to organizing all areas of our lives. You must eliminate unnecessary items in your life in order to concentrate on the important things.

If you are organizing your closets and drawers, get rid of all the things you haven't worn or used in the last year. Give things away, have a yard sale, or, if necessary, throw things away, but eliminate the clutter so you can concentrate on what you really use. If you want to manage your time better, eliminate small amounts of wasted space or activities that aren't productive and concentrate on activities that help you accomplish your goals.

Practicing "eliminating and concentrating" will help you focus your time and attention on your top priorities. It can also make your house, your desk at work, and your wardrobe more attractive. You learn to simplify as you organize.

3. **Get a notebook and use it.** A notebook that is used correctly can be invaluable to the disciplined woman. I have known women who bought expensive notebooks, organized them, and then left them on the shelf, and they wonder why they aren't more disciplined! To be effective in helping you become more organized, a notebook must be used daily.

How does it work? Invest a few dollars in a notebook that is about the size of your Bible (not too big and bundlesome), paper, dividers, and a small calendar.

The way your notebook is organized will depend on your own needs. In my notebook I have eight divisions which include a calendar, goals, Bible class notes, family and friends, prayers, quiet time notes, sermons and special lessons. We will discuss the calendar and goals sections later in this chapter.

In the section called "Bible Class Notes," I keep the notes I take in Bible class. This helps me study for the class at home and keeps notes from being on all sizes of paper and scattered everywhere.

The section called "Family & Friends" contains a list of gift ideas for members of the family and close friends. (If you write down things you hear people say they want or need all year, it can simplify your Christmas shopping.) I also keep in this section a list of newcomers at church and a list of people we need to have in our home. This is also a good place to file a budget and ideas for special family times.

The "Prayer" section of my notebook contains my prayer lists. It's so convenient to write down prayer requests if you have a notebook. I keep prayer lists over long periods of time so I can continually go back and check off prayers that have been answered. At times I have handwritten prayers and placed them in my notebook.

"Quiet Time Notes" is a section where I can write notes from my own personal Bible study. It's a good place to keep special verses, quotations and questions that need to be answered.

The next two sections, "Sermons" and "Special Lessons," are where I keep notes from sermons and lessons at women's retreats and seminars. (I'm afraid I haven't taken many sermon notes since Jonathan was born. It's hard to take notes with a squirming little boy in your lap.) The notes I have from ladies' seminars and retreats are very special and I refer to them often.

Your notebook may have entirely different divisions. Organize it to suit your own needs. Carry it with you to church and write down announcements. Have it with you in the doctor's office. Those long waits can be a great time to study notes or review your goals. Use it! Use it! It can be a tremendous help in organizing your life.

Goals

One of the sections that should be included in your notebook is a section on goals. This is the section where you write down what you want to accomplish in your lifetime, as well as yearly or short-term goals.

The disciplined woman must have a purpose for her life. Her life must have direction and meaning. This purpose will give momentum to life and help her chart how she lives each day. If a person has a *reason* to live, she will usually find *how* to live.

Have you ever written out goals for your life? Have you ever thought about those goals? Proverbs 14:22 says, "Those who plan what is good find love and faithfulness." How much planning have you done for your life? If you live to be seventy, what do you want to accomplish as a Christian, a wife, a mother, a professional woman? Think about it and write some lifetime goals down. These goals will reflect the priorities in your life and help you organize your life because you can focus on what is really important.

After you write down your lifetime goals, write down some goals you want to accomplish this year. Your yearly goals should center around things that will help you accomplish your lifetime goals. These yearly goals will probably be more specific than your lifetime goals. They will keep you from getting sidetracked and help you concentrate on the purposes for your life.

It is also good to write out some short-term goals. Short-term goals should be very specific and concentrate on things you want to accomplish in the near future. The following questions may serve as a guide to setting short-term goals:

What specific habit would you like to develop?

What specific habit would you like to break?

What would you like to weigh?

What family activity would you like to begin?

What Bible study and prayer habits would you like to begin?

What financial habit would you like to develop?

What daily exercise or physical activity would you like to commit to?

What church, school, or civic activity would you like to begin?

What is a skill you would like to develop?

What home-improvement project would you like to start?

We could go on and on with questions. The important thing to remember is that goals give direction and motivate. When you write them down, you are making more of a commitment. It may be helpful to share your goals with a close friend who can encourage and "check up" on you from time to time to see if you're working toward fulfilling your goals.

When I look in my notebook, I see the liftime goals that I wrote in the spring of 1980. One of these goals says, "I want to use my ability to speak and write for God by teaching other women both publicly and privately and by writing a book for Christian women." Under it is listed the following scriptures: Matthew 25:14-30; Titus 2:3-5; Colossians 4:4-6; and I Timothy 4:12,16.

When I wrote that goal I imagined myself as being middle-aged when I would write a book. I have since learned that when you set a goal, God will provide opportunities for you to fulfill that goal. Last summer (1982) Tom Estes, one of the elders where we worship, called and asked if I would be interested in writing some literature for Christian women.

My first reaction was, "I don't think I'm ready to write." My second reaction was, "How did he know this was one of my lifetime goals?" My response finally was, "Yes, I'll do it, but give me some time."

God was opening the door for me to fulfill my goal at age twenty-eight. I began to reshape some yearly goals to include writing a book. In 1982 I conducted the survey, read and studied in preparation for writing. My goal for 1983 is to write this book and possibly teach it in a "pilot class." With a baby due on June 17 of '83, my short-term goal is to finish the rough draft before the baby comes. (June 17 is five weeks away, and I have one chapter to go after this one!)

God has once again opened a door for me. Beginning this fall, I will have the opportunity to teach the material in this book to the Ladies' Bible Class at the Lakewood Church of Christ.

I believe setting goals makes us more disciplined by giving our lives purpose and direction. If we commit our goals to God, He will help us succeed if our goals do not conflict with His will. If you've never set goals for yourself, it may be difficult to begin, but do it. Write down your lifetime goals first, then your yearly and short-term goals. Try to be specific. Then pray about your goals often. Depend on God to help you fulfill them.

"May He give you the desire of your heart and make all your plans succeed. We will shout for joy when you are victorious and will lift up banners in the name of our God. May the Lord grant all your requests." —PSALM 20:4-5

Time Management

Many women feel the lack of self-discipline is reflected most in the way they manage their time. They never can get everything done or they are always late. Learning to organize and set goals can be a tremendous help in time management. Setting priorities and goals and learning to eliminate and concentrate will greatly influence how you spend your time each day.

God has given every person twenty-four hours in each day along with the command for "redeeming the time" (Ephesians 5:15-16; Colossians 4:5). Newer versions say "making the most of every opportunity." God expects us to use the time He gives us wisely.

Consider how you spend your time each day. You may even wish to write out a weekly schedule. Look for blocks of free time and think about what you do during these time periods. Does your schedule reflect the top priorities in your life? How can you improve the way you manage your time? Perhaps the following suggestions may be helpful in disciplining your time.

1. **Include a calendar section at the beginning of your notebook.** This section includes a small calendar as well as pages for writing "things to do." On your "things to do" pages you will write what you want to accomplish on specific days. On pay day, you may write "deposit check, pay bills, buy groceries."

Write down when a birthday card needs to be mailed, a visit needs to be made, a lesson prepared, a gift bought — everything that needs to be accomplished. It is such a good feeling to look at your list of things to do and mark off all the things you accomplish each day. It will boost your self-esteem! Be careful not to overplan or crowd too many things into one day. You can only do so much in twenty-four hours.

2. **Learn to plan ahead.** This can relieve a lot of stress and frustration. Write on your calendar all up-coming events, birthdays to be remembered, appointments, etc. You may want to place a calendar by your telephone as well as have one in your notebook. Use your calendar to plan ahead.

If you have a covered dish meal at church on Sunday and you know Saturday is going to be a busy day, then cook for the meal on Friday. Write it down on your "things to do" pages. If company is coming to visit for several days, plan your menus in advance. Have your groceries already on hand and freeze any dishes that might be prepared ahead of time. If you teach a Sunday school class, don't wait until Saturday night to prepare for the class. Begin preparing early in the week. Put it on your "things to do" pages.

Allow your calendar and your "things to do" pages to work together and be your friend. Planning ahead and carrying out those plans will help you overcome the problem of procrastination.

3. **Don't become sidetracked away from the important things.** Satan is so effective in finding ways to distract us and keep us from accomplishing our goals. There have been so many times when I have sat down to write on this book and it would seem Satan would be right there, saying, "You need to wash diapers. The dishes are dirty. Watch TV a little while." He tempts us to neglect the important things by distracting us with the many little urgent things.

I know a preacher who makes a list of things to do each day. Beside each item he places a number. Those items with a 1 beside them are things that must be done that day. He sets out to accomplish them first. He next accomplishes the items with a 2 beside them because they are next in importance. The items with a 3 are things he hopes to accomplish but may be done another day if there is not time. He says this system keeps him from getting sidetracked and it helps him focus on the most important things.

4. **Use small amounts of time wisely.** We all have five to fifteen minutes of time where we may be tempted to dawdle or just sit and watch TV. These time periods can be used to accomplish a lot or little things, such as writing a note or card, doing our nails, reviewing notes from Bible class, looking over our calendars, reading part of a book, sewing on a button... Get the idea?

Using our small amounts of time wisely leaves more time to accomplish the really important things. It may be helpful to get up in the morning fifteen to thirty minutes earlier. That extra time may help you get much more done. Proverbs 20:13 teaches us not to love sleep. It takes real discipline to rise early and to get up as soon as the clock goes off, but it may give us that time we've been looking for to pray and study or accomplish another important task.

Conclusion

I remember speaking at a ladies' seminar when I was expecting our first child. I talked a great deal about self-discipline. When I finished, an older sister in Christ came up and said, "You talk about being disciplined now, but I want to hear what you have to say about it after you have children." Having a child did make a difference. I can't accomplish as many things in a day as I could before and plans may have to be changed because of a sick child or his need for extra attention. But now, more than ever, I see the need for self-discipline.

There is even a greater need now for organization, goals, and wise use of time. These things can help us focus on the real priorities in our lives. We feel better about ourselves because we are accomplishing God's purposes in our lives. Self-discipline and self-esteem go hand-in-hand.

For Thought & Discussion

▦ 1. Do you consider yourself to be a self-disciplined woman? How does this affect your self-esteem?

▦ 2. Read II Timothy 2:7. How does God help us achieve the power of self-discipline?

▦ 3. Have a sharing time where women share some secrets of their self-discipline. Discuss how we can see the evidence of self-discipline in others' lives.

▦ 4. Take time to write out the priorities in your life. Then list some things you can eliminate in order to concentrate on these priorities.

▦ 5. Why should lifetime goals be set before yearly or short-term goals? Study the following scriptures and discuss how they relate to setting goals: Jeremiah 29:11-13; Psalm 138:8; Proverbs 16:3; II Corinthians 5:9; Philippians 4:13.

▦ 6. Have each class member share one goal they have set for themselves. Discuss how we can encourage one another to meet these goals.

▦ 7. Give examples of how Jesus planned ahead; how He used His time wisely; how He practiced self-discipline.

13

I Love Me Because...

We have spent twelve chapters discussing the Christian woman's self-esteem. In these chapters we have tried to examine what causes women to have a poor self-esteem and study some ways we can overcome these self-esteem destroyers. We have also examined influences that cause women to have a good self-esteem. Hopefully, we learned ways to improve our own self-esteem as well as ways we can help build self-esteem in others.

Why have we taken time to try to improve our self-esteem? Has it been to boost our egos and our pride? Certainly not! Sylvia Hickman said in a lesson on *Woman—Her Self Worth*, "High self-esteem is not noisy conceit. It is a quiet sense of self-respect; a feeling of self-worth. When you have it deep inside, you are glad you are you!"

Throughout this study I have tried to teach that a high self-esteem is not really based on "self" at all. For the Christian woman, a high self-esteem is based on what God has done for us and on our relationship with God. A good self-esteem is actually **denying self** and replacing it with God's love (Luke 9:23-24).

II Corinthians 5 beautifully teaches why a Christian can and should have a good self-esteem. Take time right now to read the entire chapter. It's about newness in Christ.

A New Creation

"Therefore, if anyone is in Christ, he is a new creation; the old has gone, the new has come" (verse 17).

We can have a good self-esteem because once we are baptized into Christ we begin life anew. It doesn't matter if our early family background was bad or if our past is scarred with sin and guilt. In Christ, the past is forgotten. We can begin again.

Sometimes we feel like, "If I could just start over I wouldn't make the same mistakes. I would feel so much better if I could start things out right." Well, here's your chance. Start feeling better. Remember that Christ gave you a new life.

A New Goal

"So we make it our goal to please Him, whether we are at home in the body or away from it" (verse 9).

We discussed in Chapter 12 the importance of setting goals and how our goals can motivate us and give direction to our lives. Paul told the Corinthians that as Christians their new goal was to please the Lord. Paul goes on to say in verses 14 and 15 that it is Christ's love that motivates us. We no longer live for self, but live for Christ because He died for us! It is staggering to think that someone loved me enough to die for me, a sinner.

If our goal is to please Christ, it will give direction to our role as a wife, a mother, a working woman, a Bible teacher, a neighbor, etc. We will try to do our best in every role and bring glory to God rather than ourselves. The result will be a better feeling toward ourselves.

A New Confidence

"Therefore, we are always confident"... (verse 6).

Paul repeats his confidence in verse eight. Verse seven tells us why we have a new confidence. It says, "We live by faith, not by sight." What a self-esteem builder these verses are for the woman who has always lacked self-confidence! Now you can and must be confident, but your confidence comes from your faith in God.

(Read II Corinthians 3:2-6.) Your faith in God and His ability to guide and change your life will improve your self-confidence. It will help you feel better-equipped to do His work and make you feel more useful in His kingdom.

A New Job

"We are therefore Christ's ambassadors, as though God were making his appeal through us" (verse 20).

You may not think much of yourself, but if you are a Christian, God thinks enough of you to make you His ambassador, His representative, to a world of sin. He made every Christian a minister of reconciliation (verses 18-20).

Paul said, "Since, then, we know what it is to fear the Lord, we try to persuade men" (verse 11). When we become Christians, we take a new job. We feel better about ourselves, and we want to tell others. Christ's love is not a secret to be kept to ourselves. There is a world hungering to hear how Christ can change and motivate their lives. God's evaluation, not ours, is the key, and God has judged every Christian worthy to carry the gospel to the world even though we're not perfect. It was not even to the angels He gave this glorious task.

A New Outlook

"So from now on we regard no one from a worldly point of view" (verse 16).

A new life in Christ not only can change our feelings toward ourselves, but it can change the way we view others. We no longer look at others as just people, but as souls. We look past their appearances and superficial natures and see people's needs, feelings, and desires.

As sisters in Christ, we have the responsibility to build the self-esteem of our Christian family by helping them grow in Christ. We need to be telling them, "I need you," "I love you," "I know you can do it." As an ambassador for Christ, we have the responsibility to lead the lost to Jesus by showing them we care, we love them, and we are concerned for their souls. God has given us the confidence to do His work.

Re-Evaluate

At the end of a study, I like to stop and re-evaluate my life spiritually. Paul wrote in II Corinthians 13:5, "Examine yourselves to see whether you are in the faith; test yourselves. Do you not realize that Christ Jesus is in you — unless, of course, you fail the test?"

Sometimes we need to sit and test ourselves to see if we are growing in the Lord. The conclusion of a study is a good time to ask yourself the following questions:

- *Have I gained any Bible knowledge from this study?*

- *Have I grown in my personal relationship with God throughout this study?*

- *What practical applications have I made in my life during this study?*

- *Has this study improved my relationship with my Christian family* (the church)?

- *Did I put forth the effort to get the most from this study that I could have?*

It may be helpful to go back to the questionnaire in Chapter 1 and look at how you answered the questions. Take time to re-evaluate your self-esteem. Has it improved throughout this study? If it has, what has helped to improve your self-esteem?

Making some commitments can also be a part of examining yourself. Sit down and privately make some commitments to God and pray about them. Ask God to help you overcome the self-esteem destroyers that confront you. Commit yourself to build a stronger relationship with God and to grow in faith and confidence. You may also want to make a commitment to be more effective in building self-esteem in others. Find ways to praise and encourage one another and help each other grow in faith and love.

Conclusion

It has been my prayer as I have written this book that this study will benefit Christian women and make us more useful and successful servants of God. I hope you feel good about yourself because of God's love for you. A high self-esteem not only makes us more productive in God's kingdom but it has other benefits as well. Women with high self-esteem tend to have fewer illnesses, are happier and are more successful. They also tend to make better decisions and have a better family life than those of low self-esteem. A high self-esteem helps you feel more confident, secure, competent and valuable to others. I hope you experience these benefits.

> Heavenly Father, You have demonstrated your love for us in so many ways. You gave us the gift of life—both physically and spiritually. You have forgiven us and allowed us to be your children. Because of you, Father, we are someone special.
>
> Help us, O Lord, to grow in our love for You and in our confidence in Your Word. May our lives and our self-esteem be such that others can see Christ living in us. Teach us how to build one another up in faith and love. May we never stop growing in faith, hope, and love.
>
> Thank you, God, for giving us a reason to feel good about ourselves. Thank you for being our God.
>
> In Jesus' Name, Amen

For Thought & Discussion

1. Have a special sharing session and discuss the following:
   —What have you benefited from the most in this study?
   —What are some practical applications you have put into practice?
   —What are some scriptures that have come to mean a lot to you and helped build your self-esteem?
   —What is one commitment you have made?

2. If you have the results of your class's survey in Chapter 1, compare the self-esteem ratings from the beginning of this study with ratings at the end of this study.

3. What can congregations do to help improve their members' self-esteem?

4. Read II Corinthians 3:1-6. Discuss what it means to have confidence and competence in Christ.

5. Compare the old and new life of the Christian (II Corinthians 5:17). How does this affect our self-esteem? How does being in Christ affect our goals and the way we view others?

Appendix I

—————————RESULTS OF SURVEY ON SELF-ESTEEM—————————

1. On a scale of 1 to 10 rate your own self-concept.

	POOR			AVERAGE			VERY HIGH		
RATING:	1	2	3	4	5	6	7	8	9	10
ANSWER:	0%	.5%	2%	3%	16%	18%	23%	29%	7%	1%

2. Which of the following has had the greatest influence on helping you have a good self-concept? (Rate your top three answers.)

INFLUENCE	LISTED IN THE TOP 3	LISTED AS NUMBER 1
1. Good relationship with God	27%	41%
2. Early family background	18%	30%
3. Praise and encouragement from others	18%	13%
4. Present family situation	14%	9%
5. Intelligence, competence, education	10%	1%
6. Acceptance, security	9%	5%
7. Financial security	3%	1%
8. Appearance, beauty	3%	0%

3. Which of the following has had the greatest influence on causing you to have a poor self-concept? (Rate your top three answers).

INFLUENCE	LISTED IN TOP 3	LISTED AS NUMBER 1
1. Guilt, anxiety, fear	24%	24%
2. Criticism, lack of encouragement	22%	21%
3. The world's values	16%	18%
4. Early family background	10%	9%
5. Appearance	9%	7%
6. Rejection	7%	12%
7. Poor relationship with God	7%	5%
8. Present family situation	5%	3%

4. What person or people have contributed the most to help you build a good self-concept?

PEOPLE	LISTED IN TOP 2	LISTED AS NUMBER 1
1. Parents	29%	47%
2. Christian friends	37%	27%
3. Husband	22%	26%
4. Children	12%	0%

5. What person or people have contributed the most to cause you to have a poor self-concept?

PEOPLE	PERCENTAGE OF TIMES RATED IN THE TOP 2
1. Non-Christian friends	34%
2. Media	21%
3. Associates at work or school	20%
4. Parents	12%
5. Christian friends	6%
6. Husband	5%
7. Children	2%

6. I engage in personal prayer and Bible study:

| AMOUNT OF BIBLE STUDY | SELF-CONCEPT RATING | | |
	Very High 8-10	Average 5-7	Poor 1-4
1. Daily	57%	36%	18%
2. Several times a week	33%	40%	18%
3. Weekly	4%	12%	18%
4. Seldom	5%	12%	36%
5. Never	0%	0%	9%

7. Does age affect self-concept?

| AGE | SELF-CONCEPT RATING | | |
	Very High 8-10	Average 5-7	Poor 1-4
1. Under 20 years (19%)	38%	60%	2%
2. 20-40 years (51%)	36%	56%	8%
3. 40-60 years (25%)	48%	48%	4%
4. 60-plus years (6%)	41%	59%	0%

8. Does marital status affect self-concept?

| MARITAL STATUS | SELF-CONCEPT RATING | | |
	Very High 8-10	Average 5-7	Poor 1-4
1. Single	42%	54%	4%
2. Married	44%	50%	6%
3. Widowed	20%	60%	20%
4. Divorced	20%	80%	0%

9. Does working status affect self-concept?

| WORKING STATUS | SELF-CONCEPT RATING | | |
	Very High 8-10	Average 5-7	Poor 1-4
1. Homemaker	39%	54%	6%
2. Work outside home	39%	53%	4%
3. Student	32%	60%	6%

THE KEY TO SELF-ESTEEM
by Joe R. Barnett

"We become somebody precisely at the point where we recognize that God makes us somebody."

Charlie Brown, of "Peanuts" comic strip fame, is known as the classic loser. He pitches for the baseball team that never wins. When he represents his school in the spelling competition everyone knows how it will turn out, because Charlie Brown is a loser. It is no better socially. Charlie Brown keeps trying to earn the admiration and respect of others, but every attempt to be an achiever ends in disaster.

Yet we like Charlie Brown. I suspect his popularity comes from the fact that we see a bit of ourselves in this perennial loser. From our earliest days we are conditioned to believe the only way to be happy is to excel.

Recognition is reserved for the achievers. So, like Charlie Brown, we fantasize about rising to the top. But most of us remain in the category labeled "average."

What happens to all the Charlie Browns who face defeat after defeat? They grow up suffering with feelings of inferiority and insignificance. What they feel about *themselves* is largely determined by what *others* feel about them. If others consider them losers they grow up believing they are worthless.

Psychologists tell us one of our deepest needs is the need for self-esteem. How do we gain self-esteem?

IT HURTS TO BE A "NOBODY"

Children can be incredibly cruel to each other. Do you remember the playground days when we chose sides to play ball? There were always some children who were chosen first. They were winners. Having them on the team gave a decided edge. And there were others who were always chosen last. They weren't wanted. They were liabilities.

The same thing happened in the classroom. Some were winners; others were losers.

And it continues all through life. There is the housewife who spends her days tending to important family needs — and perhaps fantasizing about the glamorous roles of others. Ask her who she is, and she will likely tell you she is "just" a housewife. A society of distorted values has led her to believe she is "nobody."

There is the man who reaches middle age locked into a job that is going nowhere. To be "somebody" is to be climbing. But he stopped climbing long ago.

We measure people by their physical attractiveness, their athletic skills, their productivity, or their intelligence. Those who do not measure up are left to a life of frustration.

Guilt can also saddle us with feelings of inferiority. Charles Dickens's *Tale Of Two Cities* has a character named Sydney Carton, whose life had been misspent. He'd had opportunities for achievement, but never had the self-discipline to do anything about them. He spent his life in London taverns, returning home each day in a drunken stupor.

The one thing which made Sydney Carton a man of destiny was his amazing resemblance to the hero of the story, Charles Darnay. At the climax of the book Charles Darnay was in prison in Paris awaiting execution. Sydney Carton arranged to visit Charles Darnay — and took his place in the prison cell. Carton, realizing his life had been wasted, seized this opportunity to make his life count for something. On the way to execution he said, "It is a far, far better thing I do, than I have ever done; it is a far, far better rest that I go to, than I have ever known." In his final act he wanted to make his wasted life useful.

---

* [This article was printed in the January/February 1983 issue of *Up Reach* magazine. It is printed here in entirety with permission of *Up Reach*.]

NEED FOR A SENSE OF BELONGING

In *The Psychology of Self-Esteem*, Nathaniel Branden says our hunger for respect is so intense that we will stop at nothing to receive approval from others.

For example, the man who has no genuine self-esteem may suffer from the delusion of being a daring and shrewd speculator. He keeps losing money in one scheme after another — always blind to the fact that his plans are impractical. He may boast extravagantly. He thinks, "If only I could make it big they would admire and accept me."

A middle-aged woman's sense of personal value may depend on seeing herself as a glamorous, youthful beauty. Every facial wrinkle is a threat to her self-image. She may plunge into a series of romantic relationships, seeking acceptance. If we do not have self-esteem we may resort to shameful tactics to get others to acknowledge that we are someone special.

We desperately need a sense of belonging and acceptance. Nothing destroys our sense of worth so much as being ignored.

To overcome feelings of inferiority we need to know we are useful. We must feel our work makes a difference. Our self-image cannot tolerate the feeling of being a useless bystander in life.

Also, to overcome feelings of inferiority we need to have others to believe in us —to think we are valuable. Such persons have traditionally been found in families and among our friends. But the mobility of our society and the decline of family life have deprived many people of this one place where their value should be reaffirmed.

The film *Ordinary People* depicts a young man, from an affluent family, who had become suicidal. In some ways he had everything going for him: he lived at the right address; his family was financially comfortable; he was a fine athlete. But he was miserable. One of the reasons was that his mother was distant and aloof. His attempts to become close to her failed. She was more concerned about her exciting life at the tennis courts than about her son. He was starving for her to say—in words of actions—"You are valuable to me."

DON'T GIVE THE CHILDREN'S BREAD TO DOGS

Many people who came to Jesus were struggling with their self-esteem. Some, like the prostitute who washed Jesus' feet, came because their lives had been wasted. They were looking for someone who would tell them they were "somebody." There were sick people who wondered what terrible thing they had done to bring such suffering on themselves and their families. And there were people like Zacchaeus who were hated because of their profession.

All of these causes — a wasted life, guilt feelings, belonging to the wrong group — caused people to come to Jesus. They turned to Him when their self-images were in shambles.

How do you overcome the nagging self-doubt which tells you your life is useless? Some people claim the answer is to simply and strongly affirm, "I am somebody!" Others say the answer is to assert yourself — "pull your own strings." But will these "positive thinking" methods really change the way we feel about ourselves?

The Gospels of Matthew and Mark (Matthew 15:21-28; Mark 7:24-30) tell about a woman who came to Jesus seeking help for her afflicted daughter. On the surface it sounds similar to many other Gospel stories, for most of them record the pleas of people who were hurting — the sick, the blind, and the crippled. But there is something especially poignant about this story. You see, this woman was a Syrophoenician. She was not born to the chosen people. This is the first recorded instance of a foreigner coming to Jesus for help.

Can you imagine how much courage it took for this woman to approach Jesus? She did not belong. She was constantly reminded that she was a "nobody."

What is remarkable about the Syrophoenician woman is her persistance. Immediately prior to her story is an account of some Pharisees who certainly weren't lacking in self-esteem. In fact, they thought so highly of themselves they wouldn't have come to Jesus for help. They belonged to the right group, they had not wasted their lives, and they were outwardly pure.

These Pharisees were a striking contrast to this woman who did not belong. When she approached Jesus He responded with what appears to be one of the coldest put-downs in the Bible: "Let the children first be fed, for it is not right to take the children's bread and throw it to the dogs" (Mark 7:27). The "children" were God's chosen people; the "dogs" were foreigners. Can you imagine how this must have made her feel? She was being reminded again that she did not belong.

Most people would respond to this rejection in anger, or by giving up. But not this woman. Her response is unforgettable: "Yes, Lord; yet even the dogs under the table eat the children's crumbs" (verse 28). She seemed to say, "Yes, perhaps I am a dog. I deserve nothing. But at least give me the crumbs." She displayed no arrogance, no bravado. She knew she was undeserving. But she won Jesus' heart. He said, "For this saying you may go your way; the demon has left your daughter" (verse 29).

THE KEY TO SELF-ESTEEM
This story is a miniature of the whole gospel. It offers the only real remedy for low self-esteem. All the modern remedies being offered to heal our sagging self-images overlook a crucial feature: we cannot create a sense of self-worth by our own thoughts and actions. No amount of self-assertion will make us feel good about ourselves. Nor can we remove our guilt or add to our stature merely by positive thinking.

The first step in achieving a sense of self-esteem is to recognize, as this woman did, that we are unworthy. We become somebody precisely at the point where we recognize, as this woman did, that we are unworthy. We become somebody precisely at the point where we recognize that *God makes us somebody*.

God does not love us because we are valuable; we are valuable because God loves us. We are valuable because He created us in His own image. We are valuable because He died for us: *Nothing in my hand I bring, / Simply to thy cross I cling.* "While we were yet sinners Christ died for us" (Romans 5:8). There is no "in" group and "out" group. He sees past our misspent years and our failures. He sees us for what we were meant to be. We are valuable to Him.

Near the beginning of Paul's first letter to the Corinthians he makes this powerful and encouraging observation: "Not many of you were wise according to worldly standards, not many were powerful, not many were of noble birth" (I Corinthians 1:26).

Paul was a good example of this. He was burdened with his past as a persecutor of Christians and he has a debilitating health problem. Tradition tells us his appearance was unimpressive. It's interesting that when God wanted His work done, He did not choose a great Athenian orator or athlete. He chose one who had reason to feel inferior. But God could use Paul's weakness to His glory. So Paul wrote, "I will all the more gladly boast of my weaknesses, that the power of Christ may rest upon me.... for when I am weak, then I am strong" (II Corinthians 12:9-10).

Psychologists tell us unfulfilled desires for self-esteem lead to bitterness and frustration. Imagine the problems which are created in the child who constantly sits in front of a television set, absorbing the medium's standards for being somebody. To the girl it means beauty; to the boy it means being athletically gifted. Accepting these standards leads to frustration, because most people are rather ordinary.

There is an alternative. True self-esteem is found in Christ, who says, "You are accepted." In Him life counts for something. You are valuable.

Barnett, Joe R., "The Key To Self-Esteem," *Up Reach*, January/February, 1983.

Bernstein, Anne C., "Feeling Great About Myself," *Parents*, September, 1982.

Brownlow, Leroy, *The Christian's Everyday Problems*, Brownlow Publishing Company, Inc., Fort Worth, TX, 1966.

Chance, Paul, "Your Child's Self-Esteem," *Parents*, January, 1982.

Dobson, Dr. James, *Hide Or Seek*, Fleming H. Revell Company, Old Tappan, New Jersey, 1974.

Dobson, Dr. James, *What Wives Wish Their Husbands Knew About Women*, Tyndale House Publishers, Inc., Wheaton, IL, 1975.

McWhorter, Jane, *Let This Cup Pass*, Quality Publications, Abilene, TX, 1978.

Morgan, Marabel, *The Total Woman*, Fleming H. Revell Company, Old Tappan, New Jersey, 1973.

Narramore, Bruce, *You're Someone Special*, Zondervan Publishing House, Grand Rapids, Michigan, 1978.

Ortlund, Anne, *Disciplines Of The Beautiful Women*, Words Book Publishers, Waco, TX, 1977.

Stamm, Mildred, *Meditation Moments*, Zondervan Publishing House, Grand Rapids, Michigan, 1967.

Willingham, Ron, *Love, Joy, Peace*, Ron Willingham Courses, Inc., 1979.